PRAISE FOR

LET GO OF ANXIOUS ATTACHMENT

This smart book is full of practical wisdom. Ashara blends her own wisdom unflinchingly with candor about her personal experience. Readers will benefit greatly from this wonderfully written straightforward book!
—**MELISA PEARCE**, Psychotherapist, Coach and CEO of Touched by a Horse, Inc.

This is a lighthearted look at a serious subject. Ashara's stories touched my heart as she shared her journey to inner peacefulness in relationship and life through the lens of self-love. This is a must-read for anyone who has ever felt out of control in a relationship that mattered and desires to feel in charge of themselves and happy with their beloved.
—**KAMI GUILDNER**, CEO of Kami Guildner Coaching, author of *Firedancer: Your Spiral journey to a Life of Passion and Purpose*

With a simple portrayal of anxious attachment, Ashara brings to life the undesirable impact it can have on our lives. Through honest stories of her own experiences, she describes with humor how she came to recognize and acknowledge it. She then shares easy every day ways to address it for a more fulfilling life.

—**PEGGY MACARTHUR**, MSW, Certified Transformational Presence Coach, Owner, Birch Corner Associates, LLC

Simple, practical, straightforward. Compassionate, supportive, and real. Not always easy, but doable. *In Let Go of Anxious Attachment*, Ashara Morris unmasks relationship patterns of attachment without judgement and offers clear first steps towards change.

—**ALAN SEALE**, author of *Create a World That Works* and *Transformational Presence: How to Make a Difference in a Rapidly Changing World*

LET GO OF ANXIOUS ATTACHMENT

7 HACKS TO CREATE A RELATIONSHIP THAT LASTS

ASHARA MORRIS

Elizabeth, Colorado

Let Go of Anxious Attachment:
7 Hacks to Create a Relationship that Lasts
Ashara Morris
Copyright ©2023 by Ashara Morris

All rights reserved. This books, or parts thereof, may not be reproduced or transmitted in any form or by any means, mechanical or electronic, including photocopying and recording, or by any information storage and retrieval system without prior written permission from the author other than brief quotations embedded in articles and reviews.

This publication is designed to provide accurate and authoritative information with regard to the subject matter covered. It is sold with the understanding that the author and publisher are not engaged in rendering medical, psychological, or other professional advice. If medical, psychological, or other professional assistance is required, the services of a competent professional person should be sought.

ISBN: 978-1-7370459-1-5 (print)
ISBN: 978-1-7370459-2-2 (electronic)
ISBN: 978-1-7370495-3-9 (audio)
Library of Congress Control Number: 2023905159

Harmony's Heart Press
HarmonysHeartCoaching.com

Editing by Melanie Mulhall, Dragonheart
www.TheDragonheart.com
Cover and interior design by YellowStudios
www.YellowStudiosOnline.com

First Edition
Printed in the United States of America

To my beloved, Glenn Weissel. Life with you is the best adventure ever.

CONTENTS

	Foreword	xi
	Introduction	xvii
1	Commitment: It's Not a Four-Letter Word	1
2	Partner Involvement and Buy-In	15
3	Self-Care	31
4	Breathing: Breathe, Baby, Breathe	43
5	Mindfulness	55
6	Meditation	69
7	Positive Conversations	81
8	The Long Haul	93
9	Now What?	109
	Acknowledgements	111
	About the Author	113
	Connect with Ashara	115

FOREWORD

I say it loudly and without much pride: I've been married five times. The first four lasted no more than four years each. The men varied in age. Apparently, I liked mixing it up. Or maybe I just went for whoever looked in my direction.

I had a pattern. First I'd find someone. Then I would be a chameleon, learning about things that interested them, whether they interested me or not. During the next phase I'd be jealous and fearful, wondering where they were when they weren't with me. I'd call and chew my fingernails. I'd worry. I'd cry. I'd cling. Then I'd try to be perfect. Eventually, I'd decide the relationship wasn't going to work because it was all my fault it wasn't perfect. And then I'd get out. I did this over, and over, and over.

And what about hubby number five? We're heading into year thirty-three, and we're best friends. It didn't start out that way, and it almost went south too, but I did something new: I stopped listening to my mind.

Your mind is telling you that to have a great marriage or partnership, everything has to be perfect and you have to be on top of it all. If you're not, you'll be alone and lonely.

Your mind is handing you a line of bull.

This is how it looks when your mind is in charge: If your love isn't giving you everything you're giving, there's something wrong. You *know* your love is looking for someone else. You've got to be the center of their universe. You need to know where your beloved is every second because if you don't, something bad is going to happen for sure. What are they thinking? What are they feeling? You have to know.

You don't feel safe, ever. The rug could be pulled out from under you at any second if you're not on top of everything in the relationship. And that means perfection. You're constantly looking at what's going on, analyzing, wondering, and hoping all that text messaging silence just means they're out of range, not tired of you.

You're sick of feeling anxious all the time, and it's literally making you ill. You don't know how much more of this anxiety and fear you can take. You're exhausted.

I've been where you are: confused, scared, and wanting to be part of something more than yourself but constantly shooting yourself in the foot about it because you cannot see what is vitally important. To have a good relationship, you need to first commit to *yourself*. And only when that relationship is solid can you commit your heart, mind, and soul to a relationship with someone else.

Change is needed, and to make this change, you need to shut off your mind. For many people, the idea of change, let alone the idea of shutting off their mind, is scary. It's far more comfortable to repeat the pattern by driving the object of your affection away with clinging, jealousy, and heart-wrenching fear rather than believing there's something about you that's worthwhile.

Feel your feet on the floor. Take a breath. Take another one. You want this relationship to last, and it can. You can have confidence, calmness, and a serenity you thought were reserved for people in a monastery. You will know that it's okay to have gaps in conversation and be out of touch for a little while. And you will be able to do those things without stress or anxiety. You will trust your love to willingly tell you what's going on so you feel safe and cherished.

You can ask for what you want and say how you feel without placing blame. You'll learn to have a loving, good conversation. You can follow a prescription for all that and come away feeling good about what just transpired instead of feeling anxious that you didn't get your point across or thinking your love wasn't listening.

A lot of what will be shared here are things I've done to release my anxious patterns and become secure in my marriage to guy number five, Glenn. The biggest asset to getting yourself in a calm, trusting state is commitment. It's commitment to self, commitment to change, and commitment to the relationship in a way that is healthy, satisfying, and joyful. You will love being with your beloved and love being with yourself. You'll find balance in your life, and you will feel safe and secure.

It takes work. It takes time. But it's so worth it.

You're going to understand how important commitment is to yourself—and to the relationship. You'll acquire some tools to help you talk yourself off the ledge when your anxiety goes into overdrive. You'll learn to have a conversation with your beloved that involves truth, not blame, and you'll learn that it's okay if they say no because you're still worthy.

I have been where you are. I spent forty years in a spiral of anxiety that started when I was four years old. The sense of abandonment and the fear that goes with that has been my companion for most of my life. It's no fun. It's taken me years, in fits and starts, to work through my issues. I've worked with experts in the fields of relationship, Gestalt practices, spiritual growth, and shamanism. I've come to understand my worth, and how I feel about myself informs everything in my life. Most importantly my marriage.

That's why I felt compelled to develop these seven hacks to create a relationship that lasts. I was stubborn, and I had to repeat my pattern many times before I realized the only way it was going to change was if I changed. As Einstein said, "We cannot solve our problems with the same thinking we used when we created them." I spent a lot of time ignoring Einstein's sage advice.

I want better than that for you.

Your mind has been telling you that you have to act in a certain way to be in a relationship. That way includes all the things keeping you from having a partnership that nourishes you and your beloved. That way leads to tears, sorrow, and the breakdown of what you want so much: a loving, caring, joyful relationship.

I've developed seven hacks to help you let go of anxious attachment and create a relationship that lasts. I'm sharing them here so you won't need to go through years of trying to figure it out as I did. We'll be going through them in detail, but here they are in a nutshell:

1. Commitment
2. Partner Involvement and Buy-In
3. Self-Care
4. Breathing
5. Mindfulness
6. Meditation
7. Positive Conversations

So start with a commitment to yourself. Then learn some techniques that will help you break your patterns of thought and create new ones that will keep you calm, collected, and able to work through a relationship's challenges without going into a tailspin.

It's not an easy path. You must be willing to take a hard look at yourself and make changes. You might end up without that beloved after all, but you'll have so much more than you had before. You'll have yourself. And that self will attract a partner who will complement you, not complete you. *You* will complete you.

Do you want this?

Then let's get started.

INTRODUCTION

Everybody has an attachment style, but you may not have ever heard of attachment style, even though it has been around for decades. I've studied a lot of psychology and never came across the term. Maybe I was behind a rock or wasn't paying attention to the small print. Let's take a look at what the term "attachment style" means. Then we'll look at the attachment style called "anxious attachment."

When we're newly born, we don't know who anybody is, but we quickly learn faces, sounds, and the way someone holds us. It's a little different from baby chicks imprinting on their mom.

By a child's first birthday, he's got a really good handle on human beings: what expressions mean, who will pick him up and cuddle him, and if his actions promote feelings of love on the part of the other or if that behavior gets him a frown or harsh word. He can differentiate between the people who are friends that will give love and enjoyment and those who are ambivalent or even downright unpleasant toward him. He will respond to each in a way that expresses how that interaction is affecting him.

The creator of attachment theory, John Bowlby, felt our first relationship—usually with our mother or some other primary parental role model—is the one that informs how we learn to interact with others as we grow older. Another psychologist, Mary Ainsworth, did some research with children in the 1960s using Bowlby's theories, with which she agreed. She found that a certain amount of being sensitive, being responsive to the child's needs, and being dependable went a long way in the security the child felt when put in a situation that was not part of their normal routine.

But it's more complex than that. Each child is different. Each is born with their own temperament and outlook, so each child will react in their own way to the stimulus from a parent. My brother and I were raised in the same house, by the same parents, and while we are similar in some ways, we are as different as peas and pomegranates. That's more about temperament and birth order than environment.

Different experts have different views about how children develop and mature. Some believe children go through certain cycles in their life, although the timing of those developmental markers might be different for different children. This theory reasons that cycles are so predictable in their formation that it is impossible to not go through each cycle, no matter how long it takes to get from one to another.

Another theory states that children are a blank slate and can be molded into whatever their parents or society want. This theory considers hugging and affection to be coddling, which it proposes is very bad for the child. A child raised by proponents of this theory would be shaped rather than loved into who they were "supposed" to be. There would be no hugging and no praise unless the behavior is above and beyond the capability of the child at that age. And even then, the behavior is expected rather than a surprise.

Under this thinking, it's the parents' job to make sure the child has enough to eat, has clothes to wear, and does all the things they need to do to become who they're supposed to be. There is no affection and no affirmation of worthwhileness unless it is directly related to who the child is supposed to become. I call this the Vulcan method of child-rearing. It is unemotional. Fortunately, this theory is put into practice in the Western world less often today than it was a few generations ago.

Another philosophy, and one held by many psychologists, is that the parent-child relationship is vitally important to the emotional growth of the child and that it should be, above all else, loving. John Bowlby, previously mentioned as the creator of attachment theory, felt that this first attachment, parent to child, was the biggest influencer of later development. The better the attachment, the better the child could cope as he got older.

There's a lot of controversy surrounding the question of whether that attachment is a fixation on the parent or someone else. For instance, what about children who go to daycare? Can they end up anxiously attached to their daycare provider? There have been arguments both for and against the possibility of attachment to someone other than the parent, and there have been lots of studies to see who children can become attached to. The jury is still out, but for the most part, if a child feels loved and cherished, they will tend less toward anxious attachment, whether that love comes from their parent, someone at daycare, or Grandma Jones.

That said, anything can affect the attachment, and of this I speak from experience. I was desperately wanted. On more than one occasion, my mother said that all she wanted was to be a mom and that she waited a very long four years to get pregnant with me, her firstborn. I have no doubt that when I was born, I was loved and cherished. My mom didn't have much breast milk, so I was bottle-fed as a baby. Did that make a difference? I don't know. I was still held while I was eating, and I don't know if being separated from my mother's breast, unable to hear her heart, made any sort of difference. I do know that for three years and nine months, none of which I consciously remember, I was the center of my mother's universe.

Then my brother was born.

Suddenly, the one who had been waited for, the perfect child, the one who never cried and always had a smile on her face, was usurped by a screaming, crying, difficult child: my brother. Not only did he take over my place as "the one," he was a problem, whereas I had always been called "perfect." My first conscious memory is of being around four years old, sitting at a small table separate from the rest of our extended family, eating lobster. I was part of the scenery but not part of the family. My mother said she thought that might have been my brother's christening party. All I know is that I was alone and felt abandoned. With lobster.

I'd call this a "lightning strike." I believe this is where my anxious attachment started.

Most people have an experience or experiences in their life that cause some sort of trauma. The term "trauma" is almost ubiquitous these days in coaching and therapy, but that's because trauma is so prevalent. Some trauma is so subtle we may think it shouldn't make a difference. But depending on the temperament of the individual, one person's life experience that impacts them very little is another person's big trauma.

Most of us take those traumas and stuff them away. They then live in our bodies and minds for the rest of our lives and inform how we live. Our minds take those events and make stories with them: If I'm perfect, I'll be loved. I must keep control of the situation or bad things will happen. If I'm ignored, I'm not loved.

ATTACHMENT STYLES

Attachment styles are born from the way we are treated as children, and they continue into our adult life. Four distinct attachment styles have been identified.

SECURE ATTACHMENT

This person knows who they are and what they need to be happy. They're fundamentally okay with their life as it is. If they have a need, they express it. If they're not happy, they say so. They have a healthy regard for relationships and know that everyone needs a little time apart occasionally. If the object of their affection doesn't respond immediately to a text or phone call, they chalk it up to that person being busy or unable to get to the phone at that time. They don't blame themselves for any break in conversation or connection, and they don't worry that the silence is because they aren't loved. They have good boundaries.

ANXIOUS ATTACHMENT (ALSO KNOWN AS ANXIOUS-AMBIVALENT ATTACHMENT)

The person with anxious attachment is completely at the mercy of their emotions and how the object of their affection responds to them. Perfection is a big word. They need to know where their beloved is at all times. They need to hear how much they are cherished and loved, over and over. There are no boundaries. They become a chameleon. If the beloved loves golf, they'll learn how to play golf. If the beloved is into fast cars, smokes, or hates the color blue, the one anxiously attached will match these things. The thought of being left or abandoned leaves the anxiously attached shaking and crying. They need that relationship for their existence.

AVOIDANT ATTACHMENT (ALSO KNOWN AS DISMISSIVE-AVOIDANT ATTACHMENT)

This person desperately wants to have a genuine relationship but already knows it's going to end badly, so once the relationship is established, they build a wall around themselves to protect their heart. They have very tight boundaries. No one is going to get the better of them and no one is going to hurt them. This person becomes fiercely independent, and they will do what they can to depend only on themselves.

DISORGANIZED ATTACHMENT (ALSO KNOWN AS FEARFUL-AVOIDANT ATTACHMENT)

This person's mantra is "I need to know I'm loved and cherished. I've got to hear that. But I don't want to get involved because I might get hurt." There's a lot of confusion and conflict in this person's mind about how to engage with others. They seek intimacy and love, but they're afraid of getting too close because that might cause them to hurt.

ANXIOUS ATTACHMENT STYLE

As stated a little earlier, each child is different, but the science seems to support the idea that depending on what sort of lightning strike you have as a child—and most everyone has them—the way you develop will be affected. Maybe my lightning strike, which was being usurped by a younger, noisy, disruptive brother, would not affect someone else in the way it did me. But something else might affect that person to cause them great anxiety, and just like that, anxious attachment is born.

SELF-ASSESSMENT

One of the ways to understand ourselves a little better is to take a look at what happened to us as children. Whether it's a true memory or one that has become a story we tell ourselves doesn't matter because what matters is the way we interpret the experience. After all, was I really sitting there with lobster all by myself? Was I really by myself? Or is that just how my mind has interpreted the way I felt on that particular day? It's the way I interpreted the experience that left me feeling vulnerable, abandoned, and unloved, and that is the focus for my anxious attachment.

So sit back, take a deep breath, and see if there are any memories out there that want to come up. If there aren't, that's okay. They may be too painful to recall right now. But listen to your body. Do you find it a little difficult to breathe? Does a part of your body tighten up when you think about your childhood? Where is that tightness? Is it in one place or many places? Focus in on the location. You'll use that later.

Do you feel you lost the thread of whatever you and your beloved are connecting on, like communication? Or closeness, honesty, vulnerability? What does it feel like to "lose the thread?" What does that mean to you?

Does anything—your feelings or a body part—hurt? If so, what hurts?

Does your mind dance away from the subject of your childhood? If so, what comes up in your mind during that dance?

When we're anxiously attached, our bodies are giving us lots of messages we probably don't even notice. We'll go over some of that later and I'll give you some techniques for settling the body down. Even if you don't know the cause of the tightness, pain, or agony other than what is right there in front of you, you can work with it to alleviate some of those sensations and feelings and get yourself back into equilibrium. From there, you can start to appreciate that you are, indeed, loved and cherished. You have to start with the most important person out there: you.

You *can* become less anxious and more in touch with the wonderful, loving, caring person you really are. I'm going to provide ideas and suggestions for that. But if you don't believe you're wonderful, loving, and caring right now, that's okay. We all start somewhere. So for right now, what is one thing you like about yourself? Just one. Maybe it's your right eye. Maybe it's your smile or even your left pinky toe. Hold on to that. It is something about you that is absolutely great!

There are other parts, too, and as we move forward, you'll find that it isn't just your right eye or your left pinky toe that is great. It's all of you.

Let's go on to the thing that trips most people up: commitment—to themselves and to the relationship. Ready? You *can* do this.

COMMITMENT:
IT'S NOT A FOUR-LETTER WORD

Commitment is vitally important. Not commitment to the relationship. Not commitment to your beloved. Not commitment to your dog. Commitment to *yourself*.

That can be a bitter pill to swallow if you're anxiously attached because a sense of worthiness comes from outside you, not from within yourself. You look for validation from the person most important to you, your parents, your family, your work colleagues, and even your dog or cat. If they love and appreciate you, you must be worth something, right?

But how do you feel about yourself? Do you gaze in the mirror with love? Do you look in the full-length mirror at your body and say, "Damn! I look good!"

Probably not.

You've gotten used to looking in the mirror and seeing a stray gray hair or another (invisible to others) line on your face. All you see is heaviness in your thighs, a drooping bum, and ugly feet. Whether they are there or not (and usually they're not), your mind goes straight to the folder titled "My Faults" and opens it up because it's been trained to do that practically from the get-go. Once there, it puts another tick under "Not pretty/handsome enough," "Looking old," and "No one would like to be with me when I look like this."

ANXIOUS ATTACHMENT AT WORK

If you're in a profession that considers intelligence an asset, you will never feel smart enough. You're always second-guessing yourself, and you seldom offer an opinion. You will do anything for anyone, even if it's to the detriment of yourself. You're a pleaser. Have you noticed how tired you are? Pleasers tend to be taken advantage of. I have personal experience with this. We allow ourselves to burn out, but we keep going because we're afraid we'll lose our job if we waver even a sliver. We become perfectionists, needing to hear from everyone around us that we did good, that it was exactly right, and that it was exactly what the company needed right now.

In the world of work, the person with anxious attachment absolutely cannot fail anyone, at any time. If you have a boss who doesn't recognize your tendencies and doesn't help you out of them, you're going to lose it all because no one can go on at that pace forever. And then your mind will have something to say about it. *See? What did I tell you?* And you will put a tick in your My Faults folder next to "Stupid and a failure."

Commitment to yourself in your work allows you to say no to some projects and ask for help when you run into a snag. It says, "I'll work hard, but I'm going home today at 5:00 o'clock because I'm tired and I need a night to recharge."

You don't need to be a doormat.

ANXIOUS ATTACHMENT IN PERSONAL RELATIONSHIPS

What does anxious attachment look like in your closest personal relationship? Let's say you're married or in a committed relationship. You thought that would give you some stability, but instead, all you feel is afraid. You put that relationship first. You put your beloved first, always making sure they are happy and things are going well for them. You watch the TV shows your beloved wants to watch. You never say you'd rather watch something on *Animal Planet* than another episode of *NCIS*. You don't say how upset you get over the blood and guts and that you'd like something a little more uplifting. *Halloween*? Sure. Put it on!

You eat what your beloved likes and you never, ever have what *you* like. I have a personal story as an example of this. Early in my marriage to husband five, I learned that Glenn didn't much care for tuna casserole, a dish I happened to like. Because I didn't yet have a commitment to myself, I didn't ask him about it. I thought it was strange because he liked tuna and other fish, but I didn't tell him I enjoyed tuna casserole on occasion and didn't ask what about the dish he didn't like.

It took me twenty years—and a lot of work on my anxious attachment—to broach the subject. It was a cold, snowy night that was perfect for comfort food. I felt good enough within myself to say what kind of food was comfort for me. It turned out that what he didn't care for were peas in his tuna casserole. I was with him! My tuna casserole had tuna, noodles, and a few mushrooms in a creamy sauce. He liked it!

We don't have it often because it's something I crave only occasionally, but if I had been a little more forthcoming earlier in our marriage, I might have found out a lot sooner that peas were the problem, not the casserole itself.

If your beloved wants to spend a night out with friends, you get anxious. You wonder what they need that you're not giving them. One of the myths about the perfect relationship is that we can be all things to our significant other. It's just not true. But when you're anxiously attached, that doesn't even register in your mind, which pulls out the My Faults folder and puts a tick under "Doesn't have what it takes to hold on to this person."

There's a lot of doubt and hating ourselves going on in our bodies and minds that have been there for a long, long time. There's an expectation that doubt and hatred will all magically go away if we try this, or do that, or just work a little harder. The thing to remember is that it took a long time to develop those behaviors, and it will take a while to change them.

The key is to want to change. And that's where commitment comes in.

It's comfortable letting your mind lead the way. It always has, and it's kept you safe for years. But that doesn't mean it's always right.

If you listen to your body and your heart, you may hear a different story. But when you're anxiously attached, the last thing you want to hear is your body or your heart because they are vulnerable, and it's dangerous to go anywhere that's vulnerable. You operate from the mindset that it's better, and easier, to just let the mind lead the way, as it always has, to do what it's always done.

Change can be painful. And when you're committing to yourself, you stand a big chance of hurting big time.

But if you *don't* change, you stay on the merry-go-round. You continue to be anxious. You may decide to take anxiety medication and find it makes you feel fuzzy and not yourself. You sink deeper and deeper into the pit until it looks impossible to get out. Maybe you self-medicate with alcohol or drugs, which may allow you to look okay on the outside while your insides are doing the Macarena.

I'm here to tell you it's never impossible. But you have to take the first step. You have to *commit*. You have to commit to changing how your life is run. You have to ask yourself some tough questions, and this is one of them: Do I want to change?

COMMITTING TO CHANGE

When you consider the possibility of committing to change, you find there's always a competing commitment: commitment to the way things have been. Let's say you want to have a better relationship with your spouse or significant other. Unfortunately, your history says that won't happen. You've got a lot of water under a lot of old bridges, and that water is looking pretty murky. But even though that water is murky, it's more comfortable staying the way you are. That path is known. If some part of you wants things to change but change doesn't happen, it may be easier to commit to the way you are than the way you want to be. So here's the deal: You have to change your commitment.

To change your commitment, you're going to have to look at what's been going on in your life and make some assessments.

Ask yourself these questions:
- How do I feel when I give up on a relationship?
- What's the shiny bauble that attracts me to the next relationship? Is it the excitement of a new relationship? Is it because I don't have to look at what I think is wrong with me? Or at the fact that the last relationship wasn't meeting the expectations I brought into it? Were those expectations realistic?
- What does this behavior get me? (This is a tough one because every behavior yields a result, even the behaviors that make us sick. Admitting that the behavior is keeping you safe, even though you're miserable, is a big realization—one that most people don't even want to look at. But you're looking. Good on you!)
- What happens if I change my behavior?
- What can I do to change my behavior?

- What is it that keeps me stuck here?
- What am I afraid of?

You have to be really honest with yourself with all these questions. When I asked myself what I was afraid of, the answer came to me: *No one will love me. I'll be all alone.* I had to take the risk that I would be okay, no matter what. I was repeating my pattern (get in a marriage, get a boyfriend, get out of the marriage, get into the next marriage with said boyfriend), and I hated myself. I had to change that. I had to love myself enough to risk it all: the boyfriend and my current marriage.

It was not easy. One of the questions I asked myself was this: Why would I give up a relationship with someone who loves my cat and makes me laugh for someone who has a cute accent but wants my cat to stay outside? It sounds like a no-brainer, right? But the C word (commitment) scared the crap out of me, and I hedged as much as I could until the moment I knew it was time to make a commitment to a better life. It's a slow process, and it's still a work in progress. But my commitment to myself helps me through more and more rough spots.

There are a number of things you can do to help you commit.

STOP DOUBTING YOURSELF

As a person with anxious attachment, doubt is your middle name. But take some time to wonder if your mind is really giving you an answer that is in your best interests. Our tendency is to go with what we know. If you're going to change your thoughts, you will need to stop every time you hear a negative thing in your head and ask yourself, "Is that true?"

Who do you admire? Who is doing what you want to do? To be successful, there has to be commitment. Read up on that person. Find out what they're doing to be successful in what they have committed to.

LEAVE FEAR OF FAILURE AT THE DOOR

We have a saying in my coaching world: Who's driving your bus? Is it Fear of Failure? Who could be driving instead? How about Commitment No Matter What? Have CNMW kick FOF off the driver's seat and send them straight to the passenger seats in the bus—and preferably not close enough to CNMW that they can whisper in CNMW's ear. Have them sit on the other side of the bus, toward the back.

CHANGE YOUR PATTERNS

We all have patterns we've grown up with, and we acquire more as we get older. One of my big patterns right now is a salad for lunch (yay) with potato chips (my reward for having that salad). I changed to salads from sandwiches and a soft drink, and I feel better because of it. It's a little thing, but it has had some positive results.

Another pattern change (much harder) is giving up when the going gets tough. I love yoga, and I found an online yoga guru who does a thirty-day challenge once a year. I've signed up for that challenge at least five times, and it involves getting on the mat daily for an entire month to do the yoga she's laid out. Four times I failed. When I saw a day in the program that was longer than thirty minutes, I skipped it. It was so hard my body hurt. I was convinced I couldn't do more than thirty minutes, and truth be told, I really liked the sessions that were closer to eighteen minutes.

This year, I decided that no matter what, I was going to do all thirty days. I was even out of town at training for part of it and brought my yoga mat with me. I did every single day. And it *was* hard. But I did it, and the way I felt when I finished that last day was worth every sore muscle. I was doing the happy dance around my house, just like Snoopy. Whoop, whoop, whoop! If I could do thirty days of yoga with a yoga guru, I could do *anything*!

What's a pattern you could change?

WRITE IT DOWN

Get yourself a piece of nice paper and maybe some colored pens or pencils. Write down your commitment. Put it somewhere that has significance to you and where you will see it every day—maybe on your mirror or the fridge. Let reading it every day become its own commitment.

But because the everyday things in our lives can become almost invisible to us when they're in the same place for a time, periodically move your commitment note to someplace new where it will stand out and be noticed if you need to. Doing this is like rearranging your furniture.

You notice it more and it may even look new when you change its position.

To write your commitment down makes it more solid. It actually helps.

TAKE THE FIRST STEP

Take the first step: commit. No matter what it is, even if it's a baby step, make a commitment to yourself, *for* yourself. If your commitment is to have salads for lunch, get yourself a special salad bowl. That's your first step. The second step, getting some greens and putting them in the bowl, will come naturally. Then take the third step. Add delicious extras—carrots, olives, maybe some protein—and salad dressing. Before you know it, you've got a salad to eat. All because you took the first step.

TRYING VERSUS DOING

I can hear you: "I'll try."

As Yoda said, "Do or do not. There is no try."

Let's say you want to keep the area around your bathroom sink neater. You tend to leave your toothbrush out, but you want the sink area to look nice, so you commit to putting away the toothbrush when you're done brushing your teeth. *I'll try to put my toothbrush away*, you say to yourself. *That way, the sink will look neater and I'll be happy with myself*.

You brush your teeth and look at the toothbrush. *Okay, I should try to put it away*, you think.

But how does one *try* to put a toothbrush away? If you leave it on the sink, it's out and not put away. If you set it in its designated spot off the counter, you've put it away. You either put it away or you don't. There's no "try" here.

Whether you're successful or not is a matter of going back and doing it again. We're always doing—or not doing. There is no try.

So do, or do not. And be okay with either one.

COMMITMENT FROM THE PIG'S PERSPECTIVE

Pick a small thing to commit to. Write it down. Then do it. And keep doing it until you feel you've got it. You're not trying. You're doing.

It doesn't have to be big. What are some small things you could do? If you usually leave your dishes in the sink after eating, you could commit to washing them by hand or putting them in the dishwasher. If you have a tendency to just drop your coat on a chair when you come into your house, you could commit to hanging it up. If you usually ignore strangers in the grocery store and shop with your head down and your focus on the romaine lettuce, you could make a commitment to look up and smile at a stranger in the grocery store every time you shop.

There are endless small things you can commit to. What is one thing that is a bugaboo for you? Commit to changing it. And then *do* it. You will be amazed at how good you feel when you accomplish that one thing.

The technique is exactly the same for changing the bigger things in your life. You just have to *commit*.

Being committed is a little different from being involved. The old ham and egg breakfast joke has survived for decades because it is still a good example of the difference between involvement and commitment: Both a chicken and a pig participated in the creation of a ham and egg breakfast. The chicken was involved, providing the eggs. But the pig was committed. No way out for Mr. or Ms. Pig.

So how involved are you in your relationship? Do you have an exit plan, just in case things don't work out? Do you feel better if you have an out? That's not commitment. When we're committed, there *is* no out.

I never fully committed to any of my relationships, although at the time, I would have argued with you about that. I had a concept of what "relationship" looked like, and if my relationship didn't fit that concept, I would do my darndest to fix it. I would be the perfect person. I would make sure everything I did was perfect. I worried and fretted, and I wondered what my beloved was thinking every second of every day. I wanted it to work.

But after a lot of work on myself, I realized I always had an exit strategy because I couldn't be perfect enough. I just wasn't worthy of that person. It was always my fault. And there seemed to be a time frame attached to it. About three years in, I'd start trying to figure out how to leave the relationship because obviously, nothing I was doing was working.

I couldn't control my beloved, and if they weren't centered on me full time (like I was on them), there was something wrong. And it was because of me. I spent many sleepless nights wondering what I was doing wrong.

When I was younger, I almost always had a new relationship in the wings before I left the old one. That was the pattern I was recreating when I realized what I was doing. Once I fully committed to my marriage, things began to (slowly) shift.

THE HARDEST PART IS SAYING YES TO YOURSELF

If you're anxiously attached, you need constant reassurance from outside yourself that you're worthwhile. Otherwise, you feel worthless. Because of that, the hardest part of commitment is committing to making a change for *you*. But I'll tell you what, if you're willing to commit to a change for yourself, it's going to spread into all parts of your life, and that will include your relationship.

So do it. Say yes to *you*. Start with something small, and then go on from there using some of the techniques I'm sharing here. In six months, you'll look back and be amazed at how far you've come. You've got this.

Take a deep breath and say after me, "I—am—worthy."

But you may be thinking something like this: What if I make all these changes and my partner doesn't like it? Yikes! That's scary! Let's take a look at that next. And let's also look at some things you can do to help your partner become an assistant in helping you and be on board with your metamorphosis.

PARTNER INVOLVEMENT AND BUY-IN

Change is scary. So there you are, in a relationship with your beloved, and it has always looked one particular way. That way may not feel good. You're anxious. You have to check emails and texts constantly. You have to make sure you know where your beloved is and what they're doing all the time. It's the only way you can have any peace of mind.

And if there is a gap in communication, your mind goes off in all sorts of directions, none of them good: They don't love me! They're out with someone else! I don't matter to them anymore. The bloom is off the rose.

Oh, our mind is so good at cooking up all kinds of scenarios. They may make us miserable, but the mind's modus operandi is to keep you safe by keeping things the way they have been. The biggest resistor to change is our own mind. And that means the biggest resistor on your beloved's side of the equation is their mind too.

When you make a commitment to yourself, which is a commitment to change for someone with anxious attachment, your mind will likely raise all kinds of questions: What if my partner doesn't like the changes? What if they don't like *me* as a result? What if I change and the things that attracted them to me are gone? Will I be alone? Will I have to start over? Who am I without my beloved? Will I be just some scared, anxious, afraid to be out there kind of person? What if I make this commitment to myself and it backfires?

Take a breath. Believe me, you're not going to lose your beloved if that is who you are truly with at this moment. They will back you up all the way because they will be gaining a lot when you become who you really are: calm, confident, loving, and able to stand on your own two feet.

That doesn't mean they won't feel some resistance to change. You're going to experience some resistance to the changes you want to make. They will likely experience some resistance too.

Let's take a look at resistance and what it means. And let's start with the resistance your beloved might have. Maybe you start a new morning routine as part of your effort to help yourself get off the anxious attachment merry-go-round. Your beloved may see this as something really weird and scary. *Why is she chanting a mantra and breathing funny? I don't get it.* There is frowning and maybe even some silence.

You continue to chant and breathe. (Good for you!)

Because that behavior is different from what your partner is used to, your merry-go-round could become a roller coaster of emotion. Your beloved sees you trying really hard and appreciates the effort but then might feel threatened because it's all different and new, and their mind just can't seem to cope.

The two of you are going to go through a lot of emotions, and some of those emotions are going to cause a bit of resistance. Think back to when you made a major change in your life. Maybe it was getting married or getting a promotion at work. Maybe it was having a child or moving out of the state you'd lived in since childhood. What were some of the emotions you experienced?

Here are some possibilities:

- Fear: The unknown is scary, and any change involves a lot of unknowns. "I don't know how things will work out. I'm afraid of how I and everything around me might change."
- Elation and/or Certainty: You're in high spirits and feel the change is the right thing for you. "I'm doing this thing! *I'm* changing and my *circumstances* are changing!"
- Joy: Starting a new stage in life can be a very exciting and joyful time. "I've never been happier in my life!"
- Anger: At the same time, major changes can bring with them frustration. "Why isn't this moving along the way I think it should?"

- Hope that the Change Won't Happen: Resistance can come into play. "If I don't move (get married; start a new job; have a baby), I won't have to worry about creating a whole new circle of friends (adjusting to someone else's preferences; proving myself to my boss again; the baby's future)."
- Worry: Because major change requires adjustments, we may worry. "Once we're in the midst of this change, how do I cope? What should I do? How do I act?"
- Sadness: Change means giving up what has been for what is to come. "I'm going to miss life as it was before this."

There are many reasons we can be resistant to change. Here's a thought. Your beloved might be afraid that because the relationship is changing and you're changing, *you* might leave *them*.

What? This is probably the farthest thing from your mind, but change does strange things to people's minds, and resistance is born of fearing the unknown. Your beloved could even say, "I'm so glad you're taking these steps for yourself and for us," and at the same time, a part of them may be thinking *I liked it better the old way because I know what that looks like.* This is very common, and you may have even felt it yourself.

Humans tend to be creatures of habit. Have you noticed that when you go to work or the grocery store, you tend to park in the same area of the parking lot? And if someone is in "your space," watch out! That's cause for a major grump-fest. We like our familiar things: The same spot in the parking lot; the same row in the movie theatre; a certain type of dessert in the same kind of bowl; utensils in the same drawer in the kitchen. Changing houses (or even desks at work) can be really upsetting (and at the same time, exciting) because we have to find our way to the same kind of familiarity with the new that we had with what we left behind.

Have you ever noticed that? We've been in our current house for almost six years, and I still open the wrong drawer in the kitchen to get a towel for drying dishes. It's down one drawer farther than feels right to me, so I'm always trying to dry the dishes with plastic wrap or aluminum foil. What used to be the dish towel drawer is now the drawer for wrap and foil because it was the only drawer in which those things fit, so a compromise had to be made. Old habits die very, very hard.

The same holds true for the way a marriage works. The morning routine is disrupted because it serves you to say a mantra for a few minutes and do some breathing. That can be very disconcerting for your beloved, and the first thing that can happen is resistance. The effort is appreciated and your partner applauds you for it because they know it is going to improve the relationship in the long-term. But at the same time, it's new and different, so their mind rebels with an internal *No!* We really do need to stop listening to our mind sometimes. The aphorism "Don't believe everything you think" has more than a little truth to it!

When things change, we lose a bit of control too. We know how to act and react to the old way. The new way requires a different response, and being human, we resist the need to have a different way of responding.

You will probably notice that some resistance passes quickly. Other resistance may be deeper and will require some patience on your part to navigate. That patience is required for both you and your beloved.

Resistance in yourself and your beloved can be insidious because it's often subconscious. One of the ways resistance shows up is as procrastination. It's really easy to get sidetracked when we're resisting something. Another form of resistance is avoidance based on perfectionism. You believe you need to do whatever it is (like committing to a few minutes of meditation in the morning) perfectly immediately, and if you cannot do that, there must be something wrong with you. So you avoid or abandon what you committed to doing. Resistance can also take the form of overanalyzing whatever you have decided to do, and that will often result in being stuck.

You will not only see these things in yourself, you will likely see them in your beloved. Your beloved will say they're on board, and they mean it, but their mind may be sending them all kinds of messages to derail the effort.

Exhaustion can create its own resistance. It takes a lot of emotional and physical effort to make change and make that change stick. There will be times when you'll want to just quit, and so will your beloved.

Don't!

Even if all you do is one tiny thing, keep moving forward. Maybe you can't do your usual twenty-five minutes of conscious breathing one day. You see some resistance on the part of your partner, so you want to skip it. Keep the momentum going, if only for five or ten minutes. But do it. You will thank yourself, and your partner may thank you too.

Studies done on change in business have shown that when people are allowed to participate, they tend to look more favorably upon the change itself. For instance, in one study model, employees were told certain changes needed to be made and procedures were agreed upon. There was a period of adjustment as the changes were implemented and new processes were learned. Then production typically went up. There were very few people quitting and little to no griping.

That contrasts with studies in which employees were told that changes were needed and what those changes would be but given no opportunity to participate. They were simply required to implement them. In those cases, resentment and resistance were noted, and some people even quit.

These studies inform the kinds of changes we make in our relationships too. Making a commitment to the changes needed to end anxious attachment is ultimately a decision you make for yourself. But it is extremely helpful to have your partner's buy-in and participation in the change. And there are a number of ways to do that.

COMMUNICATION AND INVOLVEMENT

The best way to counter resistance is to get your partner involved. This requires communication—not demands but real, true communication. If your beloved is truly with you, they will work with you to get through this happy, exciting, strange, difficult time. Many attempts at change have been slaughtered because of resistance, and your attempts may be at risk because of it. Communication is key to getting past the resistance and on the path of change.

You're taking the time to learn some tools and techniques that will help you become calmer and more sure of yourself, as well as more confident in your life and your relationship. You can pick and choose which of these tools and techniques you'd like to do for yourself and present them to your partner.

Invite your beloved to participate if they wish. Let them know how important it is to you to do these things to help you be a better partner and how this work will allow you to feel less anxious and more grounded and easy in the relationship. Ask if there are any tools or techniques they would like to explore.

Make it a journey for the two of you. That will make your own journey much more satisfying, and in my experience, it will bring you closer together.

Answer any questions your partner may have about the techniques. They may have concerns about something being woo-woo or just too hard to do. Discuss those concerns. (The last hack addresses how to have positive conversations. You'll find help there in framing those discussions about your concerns in ways that are non-blaming.)

TAKE IT SLOW

Make sure that you and your beloved know this is something you're in for the long haul. It's not going to happen overnight. It's going to take months—and maybe years. It's a muscle both of you need to build. You wouldn't go to the gym and expect to build up your biceps in one or two sessions, would you? Change is the same. It takes time, and it takes lots of repetition to get it to be part of who you are.

HAVE A SUPPORT SYSTEM IN PLACE

It's you and your partner, but you're not against the world. There are lots of ways to get support to help you stay the course. You and your partner may wish to do some coaching or therapy, together or separately. It's nice to have a safe space to work through some of the sticking points in a relationship, and you'll be able to practice skills that will help you when there's no coach or therapist available.

If you do decide to do some counseling, therapy, or coaching, make sure it's with someone both of you trust and feel comfortable about and that you both like the methods and approach used. For instance, if you want to do coaching involving horses and your beloved is afraid of horses to the point of immobility, it's not going to work. This is a decision you should make together. And make sure you communicate what works for you. No going along to be a pleaser!

There are also support groups around. Make sure you find one that is uplifting and will actually help the two of you instead of one that is little more than a gripe session. Complaining doesn't help. Look for a group of people who lift one another up and offer encouragement to group members when they're feeling down.

Tell your friends what you're doing. You'll quickly discover who your real friends are. You might even find yourself dropping some "friends" and developing new friend relationships. Glenn and I ended up with a whole new set of friends during this process. The new friends were people who were on a path similar to ours. They wanted to have a better life and a better world, and they supported us in wanting that too. The ones who were stuck in the past, who didn't want to change, who were happy with being unhappy, and who complained but took no action ended up falling by the wayside. Some of those people were family members. Was it painful? Yes. Was it worth it? Absolutely. We are at the point now where we can reach out to some of those family members, but we see them differently, and we can love them without buying in to their thing. We know who we are, and nothing can change that.

NEGOTIATION AND COMPROMISE

You're going to be doing some negotiation with one another, and it will be important to your mutual survival in the relationship. You *both* have to be comfortable with saying what you need and negotiating for the highest and best good for both of you. Your partner should be willing to do this. Both of you should also be willing to compromise. Yes, sometimes we can't get exactly what we want, but you can find something between A and B that works for you both. It's kind of like platform nine and three-quarters used for boarding the train to Hogwarts in the Harry Potter books.

Make sure you have agreement on what things are going to look like in the future. Both of you will need to communicate what you think your life together will look like. Be real about what you want and need, and make sure your partner is too. Yes, talk about the good things, but remember that *real* also means acknowledging that there will occasionally be disagreements. Be willing to acknowledge that and be willing to talk about how you will handle disagreements when they arise.

IT'S A PROCESS

You're in this relationship together, and even though it's changing, it should benefit you both. Know that there will be resistance, both on your part and on the part of your beloved. Have a support system and know *why* you're doing this. You can continue to feel scared, anxious, and lousy, or you can go through this process and watch your life change.

Breathe. Do the processes. Keep yourself and your beloved in the loop.

Then do what is best for you. This is key. Ultimately, even though you're working on your relationship, this is about *you*. You're going to have to decide for yourself: Do you want to keep waking up at night with your heart pounding and in a cold sweat because you're so anxious, or do you want to change your behaviors to help you feel better about yourself and improve your life and your relationship? It really is up to you.

When Glenn and I first started down the path of reorganizing our marriage, it was hard. I was accustomed to keeping my opinions to myself. I was always accommodating and didn't make waves. I didn't complain about things. I just got anxious. When Glenn decided to stop coming to my riding lessons, I was upset. I wondered what he would be doing while I was off riding my horse. I wondered why he didn't care enough about me to keep coming to the lessons. I used all my wiles to convince him that continuing to show up would be the best thing for us. And when he refused, I shut down. I got more and more unhappy. I rearranged my lessons so I would be taking them at a time that didn't interfere with any of our time together.

The things I did to make myself feel better and not complain were chaotic and crazy. And all it did was make me feel worse, more anxious, more frightened, and more convinced that this was a flaw on my part that would drive us apart. I was afraid that if I was "difficult" or expressed my opinion, he would run the other way.

Nothing could have been further from the truth. I couldn't see what was right in front of my nose: He actually liked me for *me*. He thought I had a sense of humor. He thought I was sweet and sexy. And he thought I had all the things he was looking for in a mate. He wasn't going anywhere.

It took a lot on my part to trust that. As we started working through our relationship, I cringed every time I said or did something that caused him some upset or when we occasionally argued with one another. I didn't know how to argue because I had almost no experience with it. I was convinced that *this time* he would pack up and leave. He never did, and we always worked through the difficulty. He was with me on this self-improvement thing, and he went on the same journey for himself. Talk about fun times!

He's not perfect (thank goodness), and neither am I, and we spent a lot of time figuring out what was going to work for us and keep us together. The biggest thing we had was our promise that neither of us would get out of the marriage alive—and murder was not an option, so we had to figure out how to be happy together or spend our lives in misery.

Neither of us cared for the misery option, so we changed and we grew. We can have a dustup now with no fear of the other packing bags and leaving behind the spouse and all the furry children. It's not just a matter of cooling off. It's more about leaning into any resistance we have and busting through to the other side.

More than thirty years in, we still have our moments. It's a never-ending process. We recently had an argument about what, boiled down, could be called our "love languages." The details aren't important here. What *is* important is that there were missed signals, miscommunication, and faulty assumptions. I got snarky. He was offended. Bark, bark, bark. We did not employ the positive conversation form we'll discuss later.

In the past, I would have started looking for the next relationship because I believed it was all my fault and I wasn't worthy of this guy. Better to find someone else. This was how my mind used to work. All the anxiety, checking, hoping, trying to make it right, and needing to know I was an okay person resulted in my quitting and running away when I didn't get the feedback I craved. Did I ever ask for what I wanted or needed? Of course not. That was not my job. My job was to keep us together at all costs and make sure he was happy, which meant keeping constant tabs on him and being scared when we didn't instantly connect.

Anyone who is in a good, committed, long-term relationship will tell you it is not all sunshine and sunflowers. I can now tell you this. It took me a long time to come to this realization, but it's true. The point is to get past the upset, come back together, talk about it, and work it out. That's what we did.

Your beloved wants you to succeed. By keeping them involved in the process of your metamorphosis from anxious attachment to secure attachment, you will have your partner's wholehearted support. Keep in mind that you can do this, and your beloved, your true beloved, is right there with you.

Let's move on to some of the things you can do for yourself to help you be less anxious and more secure in yourself and in your relationship. We'll start with things you can do that might seem selfish but are actually self-care.

SELF-CARE

What do you think is the most important thing about changing your life? Who do you spend most of your time focused on? Is it your beloved, or is it you?

It has been said that we can't love another until we can love ourselves. Sounds hokey, but it's true. Until you can find the stuff inside you that is loveable and worthy that *you* want to be around, no one else is going to want to be around you long-term. I would never have believed that a little confidence would make me more interesting, but it does. And it all comes down to—dare I say—putting yourself first.

The concept of putting yourself first has gotten a really bad rap over the years because it is assumed that when we do that, we're being selfish and thoughtless. But putting yourself first is neither. Selfishness involves being wrapped up in your own interests and needs while disregarding the interests and needs of others.

As any flight attendant knows, if there is an emergency on an airplane that deploys the oxygen mask, the appropriate response for a parent is to put their own mask on first. Once they've done that, they can then help the child sitting next to them. Why? Because a lack of oxygen can cause disorientation and impaired judgment. Putting their own mask on first is not disregarding the needs of the child. On the contrary, it could be said that it is a loving, thoughtful thing to do that will actually help protect the child.

In the same way, putting yourself first when it comes to self-care benefits your partner because until you can like, love, and look after yourself, you have far less to give others in your life, including your beloved partner.

Let's abandon the notion that putting yourself first is selfish and thoughtless. An example might illustrate the difference between putting yourself first and being thoughtless. You have an appointment with someone, and it turns out that the day and time of that appointment is going to be at a really bad time for you. When you first made the appointment, it was okay, but something has happened that's changed things. Instead of Wednesday, it would really be better if the appointment were on Friday.

There are three things you can do:

1. You could leave the appointment as it is and suffer the consequences. The person you're meeting gets to have the meeting, but you're not at the top of your game, and the conversation could suffer as a result. Being a pleaser, you do what you said you would. That may not be the best solution.

2. You could blow it off entirely. You just don't show, or you don't answer your phone, or you hide out. No conflict, and you didn't want to talk to that person anyway. This is thoughtless. You've given no thought whatsoever to how you're affecting the other person, and you've left them hanging.
3. You could contact the other person and tell them the truth: Something has come up, and you would like to reschedule. Provide a few different options. This is putting yourself first because you're taking care of yourself. You're also taking care of the other person, asking them to work with you to change the appointment to a time that is mutually good for the two of you and keeping the lines of communication open.

As you can see, putting yourself first isn't about disregarding others. It's about considering your own needs, as well as honoring the other person. I've never been in a situation where someone wasn't willing to work with me to change something around or do something differently because I was worn out, burned out, or just overwhelmed with too many other things pushing into my life. People are inherently nice, even though that's hard to believe sometimes based on what we see in social media and the news. I suggest watching less news and paying more attention to the people around you. You'll find a lot of nice ones.

Self-care, taking care of yourself first, goes a long way to calming your body down and making it easier to deal with whatever life throws your way. If you're in a constant state of anxiety, it's really hard to deal with life. So let's take a look at some ways you can start taking care of yourself. I've put in some of my favorites, as well as some things others I know really like. In there, somewhere, I'll bet are a few things that will help put a smile on your face—so you can be at your best for others (including your beloved!).

One of the things to remember about self-care is that it's a discipline, not an over-indulgence. It's vitally important to your well-being. It doesn't have to be a big thing. It can be a tiny thing, and sometimes it might be dang difficult to do it. That's where the discipline comes in.

EVERYDAY SELF-CARE

There are lots of small things we can do that qualify as self-care, and while they may seem small, they add up to behaving in a way that is self-loving. Maybe instead of having two drinks at night, you only have one. That's called moderation. Do you love chocolate? There appears to be evidence that it has health benefits, but one or two pieces is probably better from a self-care standpoint than an entire box. Again, think moderation. But whatever your favorite food is, let yourself eat it as a special treat and form of self-care. When we save these things for every now and then, they become much more precious and delightful. You might also want to consider moderation with social media consumption, cell phones, video games, and fast food.

Exercise is another small form of self-care that pays big benefits. That might be as easy as walking up the stairs instead of taking the elevator. (Okay, if you work on the fifteenth floor of a building, maybe take the stairs partway and the elevator the rest of the way.) If you have a gym membership but have been skipping gym time, put your workout clothes in a duffel bag and get yourself to the gym. Maybe you don't have the energy to do a full workout. Fair enough. But you're there. Yay! Spend fifteen minutes on the elliptical or treadmill, lift some weights, or take a class. Actually *getting* to the gym is a profound act of self-care.

Don't like the gym? No problem. You can do yoga at home. I like *Yoga with Adriene*, and I know she's right when she says that the biggest step is the one you take onto the mat. When I saw there was a thirteen-minute yoga session, that didn't sound like much, and I thought I might just go through it twice. Ha! I was done when I got to the end of the thirteen minutes. But I did it. It felt good to care about myself enough to step onto the mat.

Park a little farther from the store entrance, ride a bike, take a walk, or go swimming. There are a lot of ways to get a little exercise. And it's great when you can combine exercise with being in nature. Being outdoors can be a great form of self-care.

Sleep is another simple act of self-care. Unfortunately, sleep has become seriously underrated these days. I'm old enough to remember when a four-day workweek was spoken of as the wave of the future. That hasn't come to pass in the US.

For a time, my work commute was four hours a day, which meant I was getting up at 4:00 a.m. to do all my morning chores (horses, cats, dogs) before going to work. By the time I got home and did my evening chores, I was so wound up that it was hard to get into bed by 11:00 p.m. I was running on fumes. That was not personal self-care. Don't do that to yourself. Sleep, the opportunity for the body to recharge and reset, is vitally important to your well-being. It's a little thing, but it's huge in terms of having a healthy body.

Practicing self-love in the form of self-care can also take the form of seeing a medical practitioner on a regular basis. That may include an annual checkup with your primary care provider, a regularly scheduled massage, or an appointment with an alternative/holistic practitioner.

One of my personal favorite self-care practices is spending time with my pets. Yes, having an animal companion is a lifelong commitment, but having a pet can take you out of yourself faster than almost anything else on the planet. If you have a dog, you'll be out at least twice a day walking them (another form of exercise), and you'll have a pal to take on trips, listen to your troubles, lick your face when you're sad, and dance with you when you're happy.

My personal favorite type of animal companion is a cat. Don't believe everything you read about cats. They look standoffish and superior because they're introverts, but when they get to know you, they are as loyal and affectionate as any dog without the histrionics a dog can exhibit. And they can be trained. Where a dog might let you get away with going down an emotional rabbit hole (because they are so good at it themselves), a cat, while sympathetic, will (figuratively) smack you across the face and tell you to breathe.

Both dogs and cats have their good and bad points, and I love both. Any animal (even a snake or goldfish) that gets you thinking about taking care of them as well as yourself is a good bet. Don't go the pet route if you have any inkling at all that it might not be for you. Think it through carefully. Another life is in your hands.

I admit that with five cats and three dogs, there is always animal hair around our house, but we do our best to keep it clean. Keeping my space clean(ish), having clean clothes, and decluttering is another form of self-care for Glenn and me. Keeping our environment clean and decluttered leaves a clean, fresh feeling in your living space and in your soul. Notice how expansive you feel when you do it.

Finally, create some alone time for yourself. That might take the form of reading a book, watching a movie, taking a walk by yourself, or any other fulfilling, positive activity you do alone that is not *work*. This can be challenging because society (at least in the US) encourages a constant state of busyness and activities involving other people. Being by yourself without an internal push to do something productive can be a revolutionary act—and one that is deeply caring of one's *self*.

You're taking care of yourself day in, day out. These are little disciplines, but they add up, and they will go a long way to helping you feel good about yourself. There really is something about caring enough about yourself to get enough sleep and have clean clothes and a clean house that impacts your entire life. It's a discipline, yes. And it's worth it.

THE BIG INDULGENCES

We can look at the putting yourself first part of self-care as reasonable everyday indulgences. But some bigger indulgences, I feel, are vitally important. They're good for your well-being, a healthier body, and peace of mind.

What makes your heart sing? Is it a spa day? Being pampered and treated like a princess or prince for a half day, a whole day, maybe even a weekend (a huge indulgence) can be so refreshing and self-affirming. A spa day can include a massage, nail care, hair care, face care, a mud bath, pampering, primping, being waited on hand and foot, and maybe even some extras like a heat wrap after your massage followed by a dip in the ocean. There are spas available for every budget. Do what you can afford and then forget about what it might be costing as you enjoy every second of the experience.

Get a haircut that costs more than twenty dollars. It's a little bit along the lines of a spa day, but you probably get your hair cut more often than you schedule time at a spa. There is something about a good haircut that can make you feel *so* good about yourself. I love my hair stylist's attitude, and she's a magician with color (I'm talking purple and green). She's a huge indulgence because she costs way over twenty dollars, and it is an indulgence I'm happy to pay because my hair always looks good, even when it's a rat's nest. A good cut holds its shape. She gives great scalp massages, and her dog is at the shop, so not only do I get to see Bethany, I get to see her dog, who is the best chocolate lab in the universe. It's a delightful experience for me and worth every penny.

Perhaps what you need is just a day off from work. Yes, those mental health days are vitally important. You can wear yourself out with work, work, and more work. Or you can allow yourself to occasionally take a day off when you're not physically ill and take care of your mental wellbeing, which is just as important as keeping your body healthy.

My husband, who has been in corporate jobs for over thirty-five years, never used to take mental health days (although I did regularly), but he took one recently. The change in him was incredible. Before the day off, he was stressed to the max and could barely cope with the simplest things. When he went back to work after taking a day off to be in nature and read, he was completely relaxed and his attitude toward his job was more positive than I had seen in a couple of weeks. It's worth it. And it's important.

Maybe you need more than a day. If so, a weekend away from home somewhere you're fantasizing about might be what is called for. Do something different that will fill your cup and leave you feeling refreshed and rejuvenated. If you have a dog, you might find someplace that accepts pets, and you and your furry friend can get away together, taking long walks along the beach or in the woods. Bring a journal and a camera. Enjoy the sights and sounds of the experience.

Sometimes tickets to a sporting event, concert, or the theater are the indulgence that will uplift you. Dress up for the theater, dress in your team's colors for a sporting event, and dress like the ultimate fan for a concert. Have a meal out while you're at it and make a day or night of it.

I'm sure there are lots more big indulgences I haven't even touched on. Let your mind go crazy. What would really juice you? Put it on your list of things you want to do, and make sure it gets to the top because you're worth it! And when you put yourself first with a big indulgence every once in a while, everyone around you also benefits—just as I benefited when Glenn took that mental health day—because your batteries will be recharged.

REMIND ME WHY I'M DOING THIS?

If you have a history of anxious attachment, you also have a history of putting your attention on the care of others—often at the expense of yourself. You're flexing your self-love muscles here, both for your own benefit and the benefit of your beloved. Keep that in mind as you consider everyday (and not so everyday) ways to practice self-care.

Keep track of your accomplishments, especially if self-care is something you struggle with. Post your accomplishments where you can see them. Didn't want to get up early to do yoga before work but did anyway? Hey, that's an accomplishment. Give yourself credit for the little things because they add up. This is important. You need to know that everything you do on your own behalf—everything—is worth it and has a reason for being. And if you fall off the wagon, well, join the club! Then get back on, and we'll head on out again.

Be grateful for every little thing. Something you can do for yourself every night before bed is make a list of the seven best parts of your day. Keep a notebook or journal and a pen next to your bed so you can record them. It doesn't matter if it was getting up a little earlier, smiling at someone, or taking a trip to Hawaii. It's a good thing. When you look at your day and all the little things that make up that day, you can see how much you have to be grateful for. This is a good place to start your journey toward self-care.

And remember to breathe while you're at it. That's self-care too.

BREATHING: BREATHE, BABY, BREATHE

You feel out of control. Your breath gets shallow. You start to hyperventilate without even realizing it. Now you feel dizzy. Then you get *really* anxious because you don't feel right. It's a scary downward spiral.

What brought this on? Believe me, it can be anything. But since we're talking about anxious attachment, it could be because you sent a text to your beloved and they didn't answer right away. Or maybe they seemed a little distant at dinner, but you didn't ask about it because having to ask would mean the relationship isn't perfect. Instead, you started making up stories in your head about what might be wrong. These kinds of stories usually involve something you think you've done. This is easy to predict because a lot of what goes on in the life of someone with anxious attachment is all about what they *think*.

Sometimes you try to distract yourself by going shopping or (as I used to do) getting out the tarot cards and asking questions, but that inner voice just won't shut up: *Something's wrong! Something's wrong! You're losing control of the situation and you're losing control of yourself. You're unworthy. They don't love you. You've got to fix this. You've got to find out what's the matter.* It goes on and on. We humans are masters at winding ourselves up.

The situation gets worse and worse, and your breathing gets shallower and shallower as you suffer through your anxiety and fear of being abandoned. You've got yourself in a spiral of shame and fear. You've been here before. It's misery.

Here's the good news: All that circling around trying to figure out what's wrong can be stopped. In reality, most of what's wrong is that you're overthinking the situation.

Believe it or not, one of the problems—and one of the answers—is your breath.

When your breathing is shallow, you hyperventilate. That makes everything speed up. Your respirations are crazy fast. Your mind is going a mile a minute, making great time but getting nowhere because your thoughts aren't doing you any good. Let's take a look at some ways to slow your breathing down and at the same time, slow your mind down so your fear can dissipate and you can look at the situation from a different perspective.

ANCHORING HEART TECHNIQUE

According to Opus Peace, there is an actual National Anchoring Heart Technique Day. For 2023, it was set for February 2. I wonder if it coincides with Groundhog Day on purpose. In the movie *Groundhog Day*, the character played by Bill Murray gets stuck repeating parts of his life over and over. Bill finally gets unstuck by listening to his heart and not to his mind. That movie has some useful things to say about making assumptions, having an agenda, and being so wrapped up in what you think *should be* that you miss the true purpose of *what is*.

How do you anchor your heart? There are some simple steps.

1. Put your hands over your heart. Close your eyes.
2. Breathe deeply. I suggest you do something like this: Breathe in through your nose to the count of four. Hold your breath to the count of four. Breathe out through your mouth to the count of four. At first, you may be counting really fast, especially the holding and breathing out, but if you stick with it, you'll find yourself slowing down. Do this for as long as it takes for your speedy, intrusive thoughts to have slowed down.
3. Now consider the situation you find yourself in. Don't spend a lot of time there, but take a look at it. Let's say your beloved didn't respond to a text. Okay, they didn't respond. Keep breathing deeply. There are some innocent reasons that could have happened: Their phone died. They actually went to sleep at a decent hour. They're in traffic, and being a good citizen, they're staying off their cell phone. Your message got lost in the ether. (It happens. It's

a miracle that anything arrives when sent). One of their parents called with an emergency.
4. Get curious about the heart and its capacity to assist you in any emotional pain you're having. The heart has a huge energy bubble, and it has been called the second brain. It has a lot of wisdom on its own. Let the heart take in your pain with the inhalation and then release it with the exhalation. Keep doing this until you feel calmer. Be sure to release with the exhalation. Keeping pain in your body is very detrimental in the long run, so let it go with each breath out.
5. Now, where inside you is the place that knows this whole situation has been blown to craziness by your mind? (Not by *you*, by your *mind*, which is trying to keep you safe.) Go to that place. Soothe it. Let it know that all is okay and you're safe. Where is the place inside you that knows you're safe? It's there, I promise. Ask it to make itself known. Ahh, there it is! Maybe it looks like a cardboard box or a beautiful temple. Or maybe it looks like an actual heart. Go there. That is your safe place. Step inside and keep breathing deeply. At this point, you may be able to stop the 4/4/4 breathing, but continue to breathe deeply. Fill up your lungs all the way to the bottom.

You are *safe*. Stay in your safe space as long as necessary. That safe space is directly connected to your beautiful heart, which knows you're safe and has its own intelligence. Let your heart soothe you within that space.

Breath work can go a long way to helping you feel better. It gets you back in your body and out of your head. There are a lot of techniques you can use to help you with your breath and getting present with yourself. When you're in your head, it will go wild trying to keep you safe. And unfortunately, your head only knows what was, not what can be. It will always go back to what worked before, which is to give you all sorts of imaginary scenarios. Believing those scenarios and/or letting them control you causes a lot of stress. Stress makes you sick—sometimes emotionally, sometimes physically, and sometimes both. Your mind may have extricated you from some imagined situation, but your journey here is to make some new pathways from the mind to the body so you can let go of all that scary stuff and know you are, indeed, okay.

Deep breathing can be done whenever you want. You don't need to wait until you're feeling anxious. In fact, it's better if you do these exercises before you get to that state of anxiety. By deep breathing at certain planned times during the day, you can head off many anxious feelings. You'll stay more in your body and out of your head. Some people like to have a routine. If you're that kind of person, carve out a few minutes to do some deep breathing every day. You might want to do it first thing in the morning, before or after lunch, or right before turning off the light to go to sleep.

If you're more of a go-with-the-flow kind of soul, make a sign or note that you'll see a couple of times a day. If you have a job outside your home, put it near your workstation. At home, the bathroom mirror is a good place for notes to yourself. I used to write my notes in lipstick. It was fun, and I didn't have a hundred sticky notes all over my mirror. (But be advised that lipstick is a bit harder to clean up than a sticky note.)

Find a comfortable spot for your deep breathing. You can lie on the floor or couch or sit in a chair. Try to find a quiet place, but even if you're sitting in a public place or at your desk, you can do these techniques without arousing curious glances about what you're doing. If you can, wear clothes that are comfortable. That may be a little bit more difficult if you're away from home, but if you can, at least remove your shoes and loosen your belt. Then turn your attention to your breathing.

FOCUSED BREATH

Focused breathing is an excellent way to relax into a more peaceful state. Here's how it's done: Once you're comfortable, take a deep breath in, filling your belly, and feel how the breath expands not just your chest, but the sides of your body and maybe even your back. Slowly breathe out. Notice how it feels when you exhale. Do this for several breaths.

- Think about something that keeps you calm—maybe a stream, the wind in the trees, or even the gentle ticking of a clock.

- Now, as you breathe in, say to yourself internally, *Breathing in, I breathe in calm.* Focus on the words as you breathe in.
- As you breathe out, say internally, *Breathing out, I know I am calm.*
- You can make up your own statements as well. Just make sure they focus on the feeling of calmness and serenity.
- If you only have a couple of minutes, do it anyway. If you can do this for at least five minutes, that's great. Ten to twenty minutes is optimal.

SHAMANIC OR YOGIC BREATHING

People who do yoga and people who follow a shamanic path both claim this type of breathing as something positive in their practices. As you're learning, it's good for just about anything.

- Get comfortable.
- Breathe in through your nose for a count of four. Notice how it feels. Let the breath come deep into your belly.
- Hold your breath at the top for a count of seven. (You can count as fast as you need to.)
- Breathe out through your mouth for a count of eight. Make sure you completely empty your belly and lungs.
- Put your focus on the counting and the feeling of the air going in and out of your body.

- Try to do this for at least five minutes. But if your time is limited or you're about to go into a situation you know is going to be stressful, take just a minute or two for some deep breathing.
- You'll find that with practice, you will be able to hold the breath at the top and exhale for longer and longer stretches, so your counting will slow down.
- If you're stuck in traffic and find it stressful, this is a great exercise to help you stay calm.

LION'S BREATH

This is a very common yogic breath, and not only will it calm you, you'll find yourself being energized (probably amidst some laughter as you do this exercise). If you're wondering why I think you might be laughing, try doing it in front of a mirror. You will learn that you can look a little silly and still help yourself out. It's okay to make faces. Have some fun with this.

This exercise doesn't take very long, and if you commit fully to it, you will find yourself calming down and your attitude improving. It's great for right before what you know will be a stressful situation.

- Breathe in through your nose as deeply as you can, all the way into your belly.
- As you breathe out, open your mouth very wide, stick your tongue out, and release the breath rapidly so you're making a noise like "Hah!" You are a lion.
- Repeat. Do three or four of these breaths.

- If you have trouble breathing in through your nose, you can breathe in through your mouth and get the same effect.

RELAX YOUR WHOLE BODY

You may find this very helpful right before you go to sleep at night or any time you feel you're having an out of body experience and want to be grounded *in* your body. You might try it after some deep breathing. The two together will relax you completely and help you better cope with whatever is being thrown your way.

Do this in a step-by-step fashion. The body is divided into sections in this technique, and as you go through each section, you'll find relaxation seeping into every corner of your being. You can certainly be sitting up to practice this technique, but I've found that lying down works really well, especially near bedtime.

Even though this is done in body sections, you may feel other parts of your body tensing up. Just be aware of it, and when you notice that—say, your jaw is tensing when you're tensing your calves—allow that body part to relax as you tense the body part you're deliberately tensing. It will take a little practice, but you can do it, and once you've got it down, this is a wonderful exercise. My hands tend to tense, so I spend a lot of time unclenching them.

- Get yourself comfortable. If you're lying down, place your hands on your belly. If you're sitting in a chair or on the couch, keep your feet flat on the

floor, arms comfortably by your sides, resting your hands in your lap.
- Gently close your eyes.
- Start deep breathing, filling the belly and breathing in as much as you can. Then breathe out. Do this for several cycles. Get a rhythm going with your breathing. Feel it. Enjoy it.
- After a few cycles, as you breathe in, tense your feet. Just your feet. That may sound impossible, but if you focus on just your feet as you breathe in, that is where you'll feel the tension. Make them as tense as possible. Hold the tension while you breathe out, and then breathe in again. Make sure you keep the breaths long and deep.
- As you breath out the second time, release the tension in your feet. Let them completely relax.
- Now, as you breathe in, tense your calves. Make them as tense as possible. Hold the tension while you breathe out, and then breathe in deeply again.
- As you take the second breath out, release the tension in your calves. Let them completely relax.
- Move on to your thighs. As you breathe in, tense your thighs. Make them as tense as possible. Hold the tension while you breathe out, and then deeply breathe in again.
- As you take the second breath out, release the tension in your thighs. Let them completely relax.

- Now as you breathe in, tense your torso. Make it as tense as possible. Hold the tension while you breathe out, and then deeply breathe in again.
- As you take the second breath out, release the tension in your torso. Let it completely relax.
- Continue the process with each of these parts of your body: arms, hands, shoulders, neck, face, entire head.
- By the time you are finished, your entire body should feel more relaxed. If it's bedtime, you will probably drift gently off to sleep. If it's earlier in the day, you will likely feel as though a great weight has been lifted from you and you're ready to move forward with your day.

BREATHING AS A TOOL

Breathing is generally done unconsciously, but when you focus on it, you can help your body become much more calm and relaxed. Since anxiety is one of the things you're working on, breathing techniques are an important tool for letting go of anxious attachment.

Conscious breathing is a cornerstone in many stress relief and management techniques. Let's look at some other ways you can help your body remain in a state of relaxation. Mindfulness is one of them, and it goes hand in hand with conscious breathing. Put aside anything you think you may know about mindfulness and discover how it can help you find those places inside yourself that are worthy and worthwhile.

MINDFULNESS

We've been making your mind the bad guy in your anxious attachment journey. It's not really a bad guy. It's merely limited and works with what it has.

There is a difference between your mind and mindfulness. Let's first take a look at that. Then we'll look at some techniques for embracing mindfulness—as opposed to a mind full of anxiety and fear.

Our mind knows what it knows, and sometimes that knowledge can be pretty limiting. Even though we don't actively have total recall, the brain remembers everything—from your first breath, to the kid who bullied you in school, to the barista who smiles at you every day when you get a latte. And then there's all that school stuff: history, geometry, algebra, English. It's all there, although in my case, I think algebra is located in very long-term and hard to get at storage.

What this means is that our mind, which is supposed to keep us safe, can only keep us safe based on its knowledge of what it considers "safety." Unless we teach it something new, it will keep pulling out all the scripts that have worked in the past, which means we keep repeating habits that may not be the best for us but which the mind knows work to keep us safe.

Safety can mean a lot of things based on what's been up in your life. For some, safety is being alone. For others, safety is never being alone. It can mean that emotionally, you never get what you need, even though you want it more than anything. The mind doesn't know how to get that, so it puts you back in what it thinks is a place of safety, which for those with anxious attachment is "I'm not worthy of all that."

That's an old, old recording the mind has on repeat. You may have heard hurtful words when you were a kid like one or more of the following: "You're stupid." "Why do you want to do *that*?" "What makes you think you can do it?" "I don't want to play with you. You're stupid (no fun; fat; uncoordinated)." "No." "Don't cross the road. It's dangerous."

It may seem silly, but all those messages you heard were actually received, recorded, and stored away. If you had a parent who was constantly afraid for you, how do you think you're going to grow up? You'll be afraid of pretty much everything, and you may find yourself looking for validation from someone on every little thing.

Fear makes us cautious, so we *do* look both ways before crossing the road. But if you're caught up in an exaggerated repeating pattern, you become stuck and may stand on the curb long after all the cars are gone and it's totally safe to cross. Caution is good. The kind of abject fear that keeps you stuck is *not* good. Your mind doesn't always know the difference.

The mind also records lack of caring. If you were ignored by your parents as an infant, if they were a bit lackadaisical in their care of you, or if you were abandoned at an early age (and abandonment can be anything from being left in a doorway in a basket to being an only child and then suddenly having a sibling who requires a lot of attention), you're likely going to question whether you're worthwhile. Your mind is going to kick in to figure out what you need to do to avoid being abandoned again, and it will keep tabs on which of the things you do work and which ones don't work.

Being a problem might have worked. Or maybe it just made things worse because when you became a problem, you were told to stop doing whatever it was you were doing instead of getting what you were looking for, which might have been soothing and fixing whatever was making you act out in the first place. So you learn that to get the strokes, you have to be perfect.

Perhaps you skip the problem child thing altogether and go straight to being the one who does everything right. You were always there to help out by washing the dishes and taking out the garbage, you went to bed on time, you were bright and cheerful, and you were never unpleasant. That might have gotten you some praise, a smile, or a thank you, but it was never enough. You still felt there was something missing. So you tried harder and harder, and now if you're not admired and loved every second by the object of your affection, there's something wrong.

Your mind can take a good idea and really make a mess of it. So you need to stop the merry-go-round and let go of the past. The only way to do that is to be in the present. You've probably heard a lot about "the present moment." Be present. Be here now. It's great advice. People who do it make it look easy. You know what, though? Unless you're a dog, it's *not* all that easy.

Your dog, cat, or gerbil knows how to be present. It's where they live. It's why they forgive so easily. They don't always forget, but they're willing to see what the present moment brings. They don't think that if their foot hurts now, it just might hurt into next week. That's what humans do.

the warm place, ahh. Now they're warm. They don't think that going outside means getting cold again. I've seen cats—creatures who have comfort as a top priority—ask to go outside over and over again, despite the cold. They have no concept of it still being cold out there. Ever hopeful, once they're inside and warm, who knows? It stands to reason that outside is warm too. So they want to see if that's true. We humans with cats who spend time outdoors open and close doors for them a lot. If you look at it a certain way, this is a beautiful example of being in the present moment. They're willing to test it out with no preconceived notions at all.

So let's see what it's like to be mindful—like all the other animals on the planet.

Defining Mindfulness

Mindfulness is the art of being present to whatever is going on—right here, right now. It has roots in Buddhist philosophy. The Buddhist monk Thich Nhat Hanh is credited for bringing the concept of mindfulness to the West in the early 1970s, and it has become a mainstream practice due in large part to the efforts of Jon Kabat-Zinn, who started the Mindfulness Stress-Reduction Program at the University of Massachusetts Medical Center in 1979.

Since then, mindfulness has slowly made its way out into what I'll call the ordinary world. There are many ways to practice mindfulness. You don't have to be religious. All you need is the desire to stop fretting about the past and worrying about the future and allow the practice of being present to permeate what's happening around you—literally, right now. It's a great way to let go of the anxiety merry-go-round that happens with anxious attachment.

Mindfulness can be a difficult place to be in when you start out. After all, your mind has to learn all about this, and it's definitely not in the mind's toolbox at that point. Fortunately, the mind is teachable. With practice, you'll find it gets easier and easier to put yourself in this state whenever you want.

WHY PRACTICE MINDFULNESS?

There are a lot of good reasons to practice mindfulness.

When was the last time you had a good night's sleep? Do you toss and turn, going over every little detail of the day? Mindfulness will help you shut off those thoughts and allow you to get the rest you need to be at your best.

And because you're in the present moment, you're less likely to get depressed. Depression comes from reliving the past, dwelling on all our mistakes, and brooding over how you're likely to repeat them in the future. Depression lives in "I am not worthy."

Mindfulness will literally change your brain. New tools in the brain toolbox! When the brain realizes how much better you feel by being mindful, it will put those tools close to hand to assist you when they're needed.

You will become less distracted when you practice mindfulness. When you're in the present moment, you're not thinking about what was or what's going to be. Your thoughts are more focused, and you concentrate on what's in front of you.

With present moment awareness, you will have a stronger sense of yourself, and as a result of liking yourself better, you will be more willing to reach out and help others. Instead of looking inward, you begin to look outward. You see things that need to be done for the greater good (including your own), and you do them.

You will also be able to find your own values instead of looking outside yourself and taking on the values of others. You'll realize that *your* values are just as important as anyone else's.

Being mindful can help you recover from conflict in a relationship. You stop wondering if you did something wrong. You quit worrying about how to make the situation better. It just is, and you just are. Become present in the moment and the conflict has no control over you.

Convinced? Let's talk about how to develop a mindfulness practice.

CULTIVATING MINDFULNESS

As I said, mindfulness looks easy, but it does take practice. So at first, it's going to be a little tough. Over time, it *will* become easy. It will become more of who you are. Expect that you'll fall off the high dive occasionally because you are, after all, only human. It took you years to develop the habits you have now. It will take time to develop new habits—hopefully not years, but give yourself a break about this and just keep at it.

The first thing to look at is your breath, and we've just talked about that. Hopefully, you're practicing that a bit. If so, have you noticed how, when you focused on your breathing, other things kind of fell away? That's because you're in the present moment. If you're not breathing, you're dead. So that focus takes you away from everything except what is vitally important: your breath.

Your surroundings can have a huge impact on how easy or hard it is to be in a mindful state. If you're in the middle of Times Square in New York, you're going to be looking around, probably on high alert. There are a lot of people, and you've heard stories. You will be distracted by all the activity and all the things to see. It's going to be a little more difficult to establish mindfulness in a situation like that.

On the other hand, once you become more adept at focusing on being here now, you can be in a mindful state and still be in a fairly busy environment. Try sitting in a busy coffee shop some time. When you're looking outward, you're going to see and feel people coming and going and hear every conversation and every dropped cup. When you drop into a mindful state, when you're focused on what's in front of you, all that drops away. It becomes a buzz in the background. There is nothing but you and what you're doing. It doesn't mean you're unaware of what's going on. You can respond to it as needed. It's just that you're in the present moment, typing your letter, reading your book, or focusing on your breath. Everything else is secondary.

What is your body telling you? Focus on body sensations. Do you feel hot? Cold? Do you feel a tingle in your fingertips? Is your hair in your face? Can you feel the air coming and going through your nostrils? Speaking of your nose, what do you smell? You can become very mindful of your body and how it feels at any time, and this, too, is a way of cultivating mindfulness.

Most people go through life never thinking about the magnificent machine that is a body. When it stops working, they wonder why. And then there's doctors, pills, pain, and all the associated junk that comes with not having paid attention. If you pay attention, you can head things off before they become an issue. Maybe you're allergic to something, but you never really thought about the fact that every time you eat something with onions, your tummy does handsprings for a while. If you ignore it, things will get worse, and maybe your heart will do handsprings in addition to your tummy. This is not a good feeling. If you are alert to what goes on in your body, you will discover that eliminating onions makes you feel a whole lot better.

SEVEN KEY ATTITUDES OF MINDFULNESS

That guru of mindfulness, Jon Kabat-Zinn, outlines seven major attitudes that will help you become more mindful. They will also help you as you start any sort of meditation practice.

Stop Judging

Stop judging! And the first thing to stop judging is yourself. Whether you do something "the *right* way" or "the *wrong* way" is irrelevant. Are you doing it? Good for you! Also stop judging others and situations. Maybe you don't like the fact that some people don't use their turn signals when they drive, and beyond the fact that they are not following the rules of the road, you judge them as people because of it. (This is a big no-no in my book, and I have to laugh at myself every time I judge someone for not using turn signals.) Maybe you think having a wedding at a casino is in bad taste. That's a judgment.

If you're going to judge someone or something, at the very least, acknowledge that you're being judgmental. That's a step forward. Most of our judgments are knee-jerk reactions to something we were taught when we were younger.

Be Patient with Yourself and Others

Learning anything new is difficult, no matter how easy someone else makes it look, so be patient with yourself while you're learning. If you mess something up or react poorly to a situation (such as passing judgment on yourself for doing or failing to do something you're trying to change), be patient with yourself. It's okay. Start again. No worries. Being patient, especially with ourselves, can be challenging. And if you're trying to work things out with your beloved, you may need to have some patience—true patience not begrudging patience—while they navigate new ground as well. It's a different paradigm than the anxious type of patience you may have experienced in the past.

Beginner's Mind
I love this one. It means that you are never an expert at anything. Human egos like to be experts. Egos like to know the answers. (Ego is not a bad guy. It's another protector.) Here's the thing, though. There is always something new to learn, even on a subject you've studied for years. Always. There is always a deeper level. If you look at every situation with the mind of a beginner—a mindset of *I know nothing, so let me see what's here*—you will plumb incredible depths and find a lot of satisfaction in feeling something new.

Adriene Mishler, who has *Yoga with Adriene* online, has practiced yoga for years, and every time she has a new video for her audience, she talks about how this particular time on the mat will be different, even though she may be taking you through familiar poses. With a beginner's mind, you can feel the differences in your body. Maybe downward facing dog was simple yesterday. Today, you can barely get your butt in the air. You can get frustrated, or you can look at it with a beginner's mind and wonder what's different. You learn from the situation, every time.

And because you're in beginner's mind, which means you have suspended preconceived ideas, you are without judgment and have a bit of patience. These things build on themselves. Guess what else is happening at the same time? No judgment and patience. Yep, these things build on themselves.

Ya Gotta Trust
Do you have trouble trusting people and situations? If you have trust, there is less wondering why your beloved didn't answer that text or why they seem grumpy. Trust includes getting more comfortable with uncertainty and knowing you are safe, no matter what happens around you. Trust the process, even if it doesn't move at the pace you want. Trust that you don't have all the answers and it's okay. Trust that the sun will come up tomorrow morning. Even if it's cloudy, you know (and trust) that the sun will be there.

Stop Striving
You are not perfect. Yep, there it is, in black-and-white. You're not perfect. No one is. Even those people who look like they have a perfect life, perfect hair, or the perfect relationship aren't perfect, and neither is their life, their hair, or their relationship. All you're seeing is a small snapshot in time of what that person wants to present to the world. It could all be a lie. So be honest with yourself, do the best you can, and don't worry about perfection.

Accept What Is
The biggest lament many people have is "Why is this happening to me?" And there's a lot of angst and breast-beating about how things should be and how unfair it all is. Misery lies in that direction. You're looking at the past and

projecting really bad things into the future. Are the bad things going to happen? You don't know, so just accept things as they are and make the best of them.

Let's use Michael J. Fox as an example of someone who appears to have accepted what is. He had it all: great life, great fans, fantastic career. Then in 1991, he was diagnosed with early Parkinson's disease, and his entire life changed. He hid the diagnosis, and he drank. Eventually, he had to stop hiding from the condition and himself. He quit drinking. In 1998, he announced to the world that he had Parkinson's, and he founded the Michael J. Fox Foundation, which has raised over a billion dollars for Parkinson's research. He's living his disease in front of the world, and he tends to have an optimistic outlook.

Accept what is. Accept what you cannot change. Go with it. The old saw about taking the lemons life gives you and making lemonade comes to mind. (Minimal sugar for me, please.)

By the way, Mr. Fox has admitted he's pretty tired of lemonade. Sometimes life is okay and sometimes it's not. But always, he keeps moving forward. While he has moments of being down and feels the responsibility of keeping the happy face in front of the world, that lemonade still mostly sits beside his chair. He's a great example of living in the moment and doing his best to accept what is.

Let It All Go

One of the hardest things for a human to do is let "it"— whatever "it" is—go. Maybe it's a point of view. Maybe it's an expectation. Maybe it was a trip to the Bahamas. You can only control your reaction to what's happening. You can't control anything outside yourself, and that includes people as well as situations. Spiritual masters talk about setting an intent or asking for what you want of the universe and then releasing it, letting go, and detaching a bit. You can't control it anyway. Release it. Let it go.

MINDFULNESS IS A KEY

So now that you're more mindful, what do you do with it? Being mindful is a key to meditation. That may conjure images of a person in a long robe sitting cross-legged on a hill with flies on his face he's ignoring because he's in a meditative trance or some such thing. While it can be that, I suppose, meditation is also a way to quiet your mind, and it can be done in a very secular fashion. Meditation is a great way to relax your mind, body, and spirit.

Next, we're going to explore some meditation techniques that will keep you calm and relaxed. They can help you look at your relationship with your beloved without getting wound up and stressed.

MEDITATION

You can meditate without ever chanting om. Yes, it's true. You can also meditate without ever sitting in a cross-legged position with a goofy expression on your face that may or may not indicate bliss and your hands in that thumb/index finger configuration you see on some statues of Buddha. Meditation can become a part of your life in such a way that people won't even know you're doing it. How cool is that?

Actually, once you've participated in meditation for a while, you won't care if people see you doing it. You'll probably invite them to join you because it feels so good. Anyone can meditate, no matter what your religious affiliation is (or is not).

Meditation is a way of helping you calm down and look at your life from a different perspective—one without fear or anxiety. We're not simply talking about contemplation and reflection here. The word "meditation" is often used to mean that. As we are referring to it here, meditation is a practice for calming the mind, focusing attention, and raising awareness.

WHAT WE DO WHEN WE MEDITATE

Meditation can take a variety of forms, and you can be doing all sorts of things when you meditate. You don't have to be sitting down. You *can* sit, but if you'd rather be moving, you can do that. Maybe you're smelling flowers. That can be a meditation. A lot of meditation is about where your mind is. If you're smelling a flower but thinking about how much work you have left to do in your day, that's not meditation.

Focusing on the flower, seeing the individual petals, gazing in wonder at the stem and how the petals are spread around the center, smelling whatever scent is being sent out by the flower (and sometimes there is little or none)—*that's* meditation. You're present. You're seeing the flower in all its glory, and you're taking it all in. There is nothing but you and the flower.

By using mindfulness, you can meditate anywhere: when you're gardening; when you're drawing or writing; when you're singing; when you're sitting quietly; when you're petting your animal companion or grooming a horse. Mindfulness begins with the breath, and meditation can start from the same place:

- Pay attention to your breathing. Use the techniques discussed with mindfulness. Breathe in. Breathe out.

- Pay attention when your mind wanders from the breathing. It will happen, and it will happen often. Sometimes when you're tired, concentrating on your breathing will put you right to sleep. (It's a really good technique if you're tossing and turning at night.) Just return to paying attention to your breathing when you catch your mind wandering.
- Be easy on yourself. It's not a simple thing, but it does get easier. And remember, all those people who make it look so easy were where you are when they began meditating. And they still have their moments when even focusing on the breath is a chore. (I know whereof I speak. I've meditated for years and it happens to me.)

It doesn't matter how long you meditate. Five minutes can be enough. If you start there, great. As you experience meditation over time, you may find that you want to stay in a meditative state longer. My husband and I meditate for twenty minutes each night before sleep and thirty minutes in the morning to greet the day. If that's too much for you, that's okay. Do what works best for you.

Be as consistent as you can. As with many things, meditation works best with consistent practice. You'll find that it calms your mind and brings you into yourself.

SITTING MEDITATION AND THE PESKY LOTUS POSITION

When you think of meditation, you may have an image of a person sitting straight as a pole, legs crossed on top of one another, a blissful expression on their face, hands either folded at the heart or resting on the knees with the thumb and index fingers of each hand touching. That's called lotus position, and it's a pretty image, but unless you've been practicing lotus for years or are a pretzel, you can forget about that position.

You don't have to sit in lotus position to do the most basic of meditations: sitting meditation. The only thing I would caution you on is slumping. There's something about slumping that ruins meditation. If you can't sit fairly straight, even when using a backrest, then lie down. It's okay. Either way, it works.

Here are some tips for doing a simple form of sitting meditation:

- Sit any way that feels good to you, including in a chair. My husband sits with his legs crossed and leaning against the headboard of our bed. Me? On the bed, I put my legs out straight because that's comfortable for me, and I lean as straight as I can against the headboard.
- Keep your spine straight but not tight. If you can sit up straight without support, yay! If not, using the back of a chair or couch (if you're sitting on a chair or couch), leaning against the headboard of your bed, or even leaning against a tree is okay. Make sure you're sitting up as straight as possible. Avoid slumping.
- If you're sitting up straight, your shoulders should naturally be back a bit, but it's a good idea to roll

forward, up, and back to relax them and allow your shoulder blades to come closer together (without putting undue stress on them).
- There are several ways you can place your hands: lightly in your lap, palms down or up; resting on your knees, palms up or down; thumb touching the base of the ring or index finger; or even in prayer position over your heart.
- Even though you're sitting up straight, your neck and head might come forward a bit. Move it a little back, with your chin tucked in slightly. Think head over your heart and your heart over your pelvis. You're looking for straightness without strain.
- Eyes can be closed, looking slightly down, or you can look into the distance with what's called "soft eyes." That is, you're not focused on anything in particular.
- Relax your mouth and tongue. You can slightly open your mouth, or it can be closed. You're aiming for no tension anywhere in your body, and we tend to hold a lot of tension in our face and mouth.
- Do the best you can with the position. The more you practice, the easier it becomes. It may be very difficult at first to keep your spine, neck, and head in a straight line, but over time, it will feel natural and good to be in that position.
- Now, start deep breathing. Allow your mind to flow. Know that thoughts are going to come in. That's okay. It's what the mind does. What *you* do

is let those thoughts go straight through without focusing on them.
- If it helps, focus on a phrase or what's called a mantra. A mantra can be about anything, and it's always helpful to use a mantra that is specific to what you might be experiencing. It can be in your native language, or you can utter any of the many Sanskrit mantras. Here are a few mantra suggestions:
  - I am content in this moment.
  - I am guided to my highest and best good.
  - I am Love.
  - My beloved and I are learning about one another.
  - I share my truth.
  - All is well. I am safe. (I use this one a lot.)
  - Om Shanti Om. (*Shanti* means "peace" in Sanskrit.)
  - Om Shanti Shanti Shanti.
  - Om Mani Padme Hum.

WALKING MEDITATION

If you want to be moving while being present, walking meditation may be for you. If you can only do it for five minutes, that's okay. See if you can work up to something longer. It may take some time to get there. If you can, take ten to fifteen minutes or longer if that feels right to you. Find a quiet place to walk, indoors or outdoors. Make sure that wherever you are, you feel comfortable.

- You can do just about anything with your hands and arms: They can be hanging loosely at your side. You can put them in a prayer position. You can put them in your pockets if that feels right and comfortable to you. They can swing loosely as you walk. Crossing them in front of your body might not be the best, so I suggest you avoid that. Pretty much anything else goes.
- Walk slowly. This isn't about getting your heart rate up. This is about being deliberate *in* your movements and being present *with* your movements. Sometimes a little counting can help. Count one, two, three as you make a step with each count. Be very mindful of your steps and where you put each foot. Is there something underneath your foot that you can feel? Just observe it. No need to figure out what it is. (That is, unless you just stepped on an ant hill or something noxious like dog poo. But if you're paying attention to your walking, you will have already gone around the ants or poo.)
- Walk in any direction that suits you. If you have a limited amount of space, indoors or outdoors, you might want to go slowly back and forth or walk in a circle. If you're inside, you can go from room to room. If you have a garden, you can walk around the garden or your yard. It doesn't have to be the same every time. You can even do a walking meditation going from one meeting to another in your

office building. Just make sure you build in enough time to get there!
- Your mind is going to wander. It's a fact of life. Here are some things you can do to get yourself back to the present moment, which is you walking around meditatively.
  › Focus your attention. What is around you? What does it feel like to be moving through the space in which you're walking?
  › Take some deep breaths.
  › Feel your feet on the ground. Keep breathing.
  › Take a very deliberate step and notice how your foot leaves the ground. Does it come up all at once or does your heel leave first and your toes last? This might sound goofy, but different ways of moving your foot are going to give you different feelings. Play with it.
  › Notice how your leg moves forward. What does that feel like?
  › Notice how your foot lands on the ground. Does it land with a plunk or does it fall softly? Play with that too. Take another step, noticing the same things with the other foot.
  › What does the rest of your body feel like? Is there tension anywhere? Can you isolate that tension and then let it go?
  › Keep paying attention to your breathing.

› Continue to walk in a very deliberate fashion. This is one of those things you cannot rush through. You have to be right there.
› Focus on what your body is doing. Is your stomach grumbling? Is your head tilted to one side? Does one hand feel different than the other?
› Listen to the sounds around you. If you're inside, what do you hear? Is there machinery humming or people talking? What do your feet sound like on the floor or carpet? What else do you hear? If you're outside, focus on the sounds of nature. Apart from the sounds of nature, what do you hear in the environment around you? You can listen inside yourself as well. For instance, what does your breath sound like?
› The more you focus on what's going on around you in the moment, the less chance your mind will have to fill you up with thoughts of the past or future. You're walking. You're observing, feeling, and taking in everything around you. Try it. It's so relaxing.

BODY SCAN MEDITATION

A body scan meditation is a great thing to do if you feel you're spiraling out of control with an inability to focus, merry-go-round thoughts, and anxiety. By focusing on what's going on with your body, you can change your state and become calmer and more relaxed. So let's get started.

Find a comfortable position. Lying down is best, but if you would feel better sitting in a comfy chair, do that. Close your eyes. Know that you're safe. The boogie man is not going to get you. If you have a pet who wants to be with you, feel free to invite them to join you if they can be fairly still. I personally *would* invite them to join you, so long as they are quiet.

- Check in with your body. Where is there tension or stress? Make note of those places. This is an exercise in observation.
- Feel where your body touches the surface of whatever you are lying or sitting on. Do you feel supported? Is the temperature neutral? Cold? Warm?
- Start deep breathing. How does the air feel coming in and going out of your body? What does it feel like to have your lungs fill with air? Allow your lungs and belly to expand and contract with each inhalation and exhalation. If your mind wanders, that's okay. Thank it and go back to focusing on your breath.
- As you continue to breathe deeply, focus your attention on your feet. Where are they touching the surface of what you're lying or sitting on and is the surface smooth or scratchy? Are they warm/cold/comfortable? Are they tense or relaxed? What other things do you observe about your feet?

- Continue to breathe deeply and move up to your lower legs. What do you feel? Notice temperature, tension or relaxation, discomfort or neutrality, and any other sensations.
- Continue to breathe deeply and move up to your thighs. Notice how they feel.
- Repeat the process as you move up to your lower torso, upper torso, lungs, heart area, back, shoulders, arms, hands, neck, face, and whole head.
- Now put it all together, scanning from top to bottom. Make note of any areas that are tense or uncomfortable.
- Now you're going to help any tension leave your body so you can become more relaxed. Imagine a stream of energy flowing into your body through the top of your head. Allow that energy to flow through your body and come out through the bottoms of your feet. Keep the energy stream flowing, allowing it to soothe every sore spot and every place you are tense. Don't stop until your body feels completely relaxed. Enjoy this feeling of relaxation. Ahh.
- Stay in that space until you feel ready to come back into the present. Then wiggle your fingers and toes, move your head around, and become aware of your surroundings. Open your eyes. You will likely feel refreshed and relaxed.

This is a great exercise to do when you're feeling particularly stressed or anxious. It's also a great way to start the day. Do this as often as you need to maintain a sense of relaxation.

MEDITATION IS A TOOL

Now that we've demystified meditation and you have several meditation tools at your disposal, let's step back for a moment and talk about it as a tool for unburdening yourself of anxious attachment. Meditation (and its companion, mindfulness) can help you stay in a space where you're taking care of yourself and putting your mind and heart in a place where you know how worthwhile and worthy you are. You will be able to figure out what *you* want and spend less time trying to figure out what your beloved wants (so you can give it to them). It will also help you figure out what you need in your relationship.

But once you have a sense of what you want and need, you need to be able to ask for them in a way that is nonjudgmental, nonthreatening, and without excessive emotion. And you need to be able to let go of the outcome once you've asked. If your beloved is truly worth your time and effort, they will be happy to support you and work with you in making your relationship the best for both of you. Being in a secure, strong relationship takes two people who are committed to it. And that requires positive communication.

Don't worry. You're ready for this final puzzle piece.

POSITIVE CONVERSATIONS

"**Y**ou make me so upset!"

What is wrong with that sentence? Let me give you a hint. No one can *make* you anything. You are responsible for your thoughts and feelings. Your response to a situation is what causes your emotions, so you may become upset because of something someone else did, but they didn't make you feel that way. *You* made you feel that way.

The quicker you figure this out, the easier it will be to get what you want.

Humans like to blame others for their circumstances. But in truth, the only thing you can control is your reaction to what's going on around you. You can't control people or what they say or do, no matter how hard you try. You can only control how you react to these things.

If someone comes to you and says, "You make me so upset!" what is the first thing you feel? For someone who is anxiously attached, it could be guilt. But it could also be annoyance. And when you're anxiously attached, you shut down when you feel annoyance and any other negative emotion. You stop hearing what the person is saying and you focus on the blame they're placing on you. This is a really bad way to have a heartfelt conversation because you're coming from a place of defense (or offense) instead of a place of willingness to work things out.

With anxious attachment, you always take the blame. Suspend that response. Now that you're more in your body, instead of getting anxious because your beloved may not be responding to you, get curious.

Is it possible your beloved is not willing to open the door to any sort of conversation, including one involving blame and counter-blame, and are silent? Is it possible their upbringing led to a pattern of being quiet when someone gets upset? Is it possible they are just plain afraid of what could happen? That fear is *not your fault*. It's *their* stuff, from *their* childhood. All you can do is say how you feel and do it in a non-blaming way that admits what's going on for you.

You are not responsible for anyone's feelings, thoughts, and actions except your own. That's what we want to get under control with self-care, breathing, mindfulness, and meditation. And now we're adding a technique for facing conflict in a positive way.

HOW CONVERSATIONS OFTEN GO

Before we look at how conversations *can* go, let's take a look at how they often go when there is conflict or disagreement. Most people talk from a position of blame coupled with victimhood: "You make me so upset when you don't do your share of the chores." "You make me so worried when you come home late and don't text me." They know what they don't want from a relationship: They *don't* want to be angry, they *don't* want to have to constantly defend themselves, and they *don't* want stress and anxiety. But often, they also don't know what they *want* in the relationship beyond being with someone and being happy.

But what does "being happy" mean? What does it look like? If there's a bit of conflict, can you still be happy?

Most people make assumptions about what others are thinking or feeling—all the time. Instead of asking to find out what they are actually feeling, we make stuff up based on how we feel about ourselves, what we learned in childhood, and what our experiences have been in other relationships. Then we say things based on the assumptions we make: "You don't love me." "You never want to be with me." "You're thoughtless." "You're going to leave me for someone else."

Some of those assumptions are scary. Most of them are probably only figments of your imagination. Any time you start a conversation with any of the above, it will put the other person on the defensive. And you're assuming the worst.

So what can your beloved do? They might speak harshly without meaning to. People don't like to be blamed for things they know are untrue. They might also get quiet and go inside as a way to avoid a conversation that could get out of hand and become destructive. I'm not saying it's right or wrong. It just is. It's your beloved's way of coping, and it was probably learned at a young age.

When *you're* silent, it gets even worse. It can cause resentment, both on your part and the part of your beloved. Nothing is getting solved in silence. What if the other person doesn't even notice that you're silent? They may go on like nothing is wrong, and yet from your perspective, everything is wrong. You start to feel unworthy. You feel invisible. You feel you're getting stepped on. How can your beloved possibly act as though nothing is wrong?

Take a deep breath and ask yourself this question: Does your beloved even know anything is wrong? You're silent. No messages are being sent other than "I'm being silent."

A SHOT OF COURAGE

At these times, a shot of courage can get you what you really want. Someone has to take the first step. If you want to be better at relationships and your relationship has hit a huge bump, it's going to have to be you. Why? Because you're the one who is willing to let go of all that anxiety and work through your stuff to be more in touch with the world around you and less available for those voices in your head to control you.

It takes a lot to do this. To say what you want and how you feel, you need to be willing to *be* a number of things.

- **Vulnerable:** You don't know how your beloved is going to react. You have to be open. That doesn't mean you should just take it if you get an abusive response. Absolutely not! But you have to be willing to put yourself out there. And you need to hope and envision the best outcome.

- **Honest:** If you feel scared, you have to be willing to say you feel scared. *You* feel scared. You have to own your feelings and be honest about what a situation feels like to you.
- **Straightforward in communication:** You have to say exactly what you mean. There can be no beating around the bush. I was a great bush beater. I learned how to do it as a kid. Over time, it's gotten easier to say what I mean without fear of being cast out, ignored, or unloved. With practice, you can also develop the skill of being straightforward in your communication.
- **Willing to listen:** You have to be willing to hear what your beloved has to say to you. If the response is abusive, you have the right to stop it and take a breather. If they are saying something in an unabusive way, but you don't want to hear it, you have to be willing to hear it—really *hear* it. Among other things, that means not formulating a defense while they're talking. Instead, you're going to hear what your beloved has to say, digest it, and then respond.
- **Willing to compromise if necessary:** Any relationship is a series of compromises. It doesn't have to be that harsh, but compromise is a really good tool to have in your toolbox. Usually, the compromise

may feel a little uncomfortable at first, but you'll find that in the long run, it works out very well for both parties.

- **Willing to put emotions aside in the conversation:** This is a tough one. Emotions make us feel alive. When we experience them, we know we're in our body. But all that emotion is what caused the problem in the first place. If you're unable to have a conversation without getting overly emotional, don't initiate it. If your partner initiates it (perhaps *they're* asking for what *they* need), ask for a little space because you're not in a position to hear them and promise to have the conversation when you can be present without being overly emotional. If you start to cry during the discussion but are still able to speak from a place of non-blaming and from your perspective as opposed to what the other person "did" to you, that works. You'll find the crying will stop a lot quicker when you engage in positive conversation, and as time goes on, it might not even happen.
- **Willing to stop the conversation and take a breather if it gets out of hand:** If one of you starts defaulting to accusing and blaming, it's time to stop the conversation and walk away for a little while. Let things cool off. When you're both in a better place, return to the conversation.

How do you do this? How can you have a conversation that doesn't place blame, says how you feel, and gets a response?

THE FORMULA

There's a simple formula for having this kind of conversation. Here it is:
1. State your feelings and the facts.
2. Ask for what you want.
3. Let go of the outcome.

Let's look at each piece individually.

State Your Feelings and the Facts

There are a number of ways you can state your feelings and facts, but here's a simple sentence structure to make it easy: "I felt (state your feeling) when you (the action that was taken, *not* what you think was behind the action)."

Here's an example: I felt scared and abandoned when you didn't text or call to tell me you were going to be late coming home. Note that the feeling was *scared and abandoned* and the action was *you didn't text to tell me you were going to be late coming home*. In this example, you are stating how *you* felt, and the behavior of your beloved is very specific and factual. Your beloved did not text to tell you they would be coming home late. You are not saying, "You make me feel . . ." and you're not making generalizations.

Here is an example of the same kind of statement done in a problematic way that is accusing, places blame, and makes the other person responsible for your feelings: "You make me feel so scared when you don't call or text me. Don't you know how abandoned this makes me feel? Why do you do that?"

Notice that in the first example, no blame is placed. You are owning your feelings and taking responsibility for the fact that you feel them. You said, "I felt scared and abandoned," not "You make me feel so scared." The difference between these two ways of stating your feelings is important because it's not your beloved's fault that you feel that way. They are *your* emotions, learned at a young age, and now in your face because you've been triggered by your beloved's action. That is not their fault.

You then state the triggering action. You're not making assumptions about why they did that action, you are merely stating the action—that they didn't text or call you to say they were going to be late. Okay. Your beloved didn't text. There is no disputing that fact. That's what happened, and you are making no assumptions as to *why* they didn't text.

Here are a couple of examples of assumptions: "You decided to abandon me by not texting or calling." "You didn't consider how I would feel if you didn't call or text." You don't know either of those things. Maybe they were in the middle of a situation that didn't allow calling or texting. There are a dozen different reasons that could be in the mix, and none of them have anything to do with you.

Only state the facts. By stating only the facts, strong emotion, which is usually a precursor to a really nasty argument with no good outcome, is avoided in the conversation. Your partner cannot dispute the fact that they did not text. When you use this structure, you avoid blaming your partner. No one likes to be blamed, so let's avoid that.

Ask for What You Want
In an unemotional way, ask for what you want. Stick to what you want without assuming anything you say is going to cause some sort of emotion in your partner. Be curious. Be willing to be vulnerable in asking for what you want. Use this formula: "I want you to (state the action you are requesting)."

Here's an example: "I want you to call or text me when you're going to be late." Again, stick to the facts. You are merely asking for what you want. Don't make threats like "If you don't, I'll leave you." Just make your request without embellishment. Humans love to embellish. Avoid it because it's death to any sort of good conversation.

Be Willing to Let It Go
Your partner will either agree to do what you want or they won't. If you're in a good relationship, chances are good that what you're asking for will be given if it's reasonable. But what if it isn't? This might be a good time to look at compromise. What's most important for you is willingness to let go of any expectation of outcome. In your mind, calling or texting when they're going to be late is a no-brainer. That might not be the case for your beloved.

And that allows you to use the formula I'm going to provide to open a whole new level of conversation.

If your partner says no, there's something else going on. So let's take this to the next step. Let's say your partner says no. First, think about how you *feel* about that response. Are you hurt? Surprised? Angry? Then think about whether it's worth having a conversation with your partner to express the emotions you're feeling, and if so, how you can do it without laying blame. This is a good time to get really curious.

Becoming curious does not mean you should ask them *why* they said no. "Why" is a terrible word to use when you're trying to have a good conversation. It implies there is something wrong, and believe it or not, it can cause a lot of people to feel they're being blamed. So express your curiosity without asking why.

Let's look at an example. You have stated that you want your partner to call or text when they're going to be late, and your partner has replied, "No." Here's a method for what to do next: 1. State the facts and how you feel. 2. Ask for clarification. 3. Be willing to let it go.

Let's break it down.

State the facts and how you feel. Here's an example: "I feel hurt that you have said you don't want to call or text when you're going to be late." You're stating your feelings—hurt—without blaming or criticizing.

Ask for clarification. Example: "I want to understand. What is it about calling or texting when you're going to be late that led to you saying no to it?"

Now your job is to really listen. Your beloved should tell you what the issue is. You may have to go back and forth a few times. It's important to avoid formulating a response to anything your beloved is saying. You're gathering information at this point. You want to understand. It's important that you not let your emotions get the better of you. Stick to the facts. Reflect back to your beloved what you believe you heard.

Let's say your beloved says they feel confined and put upon when they have to call or text when they're going to be late. You might want to find out if that's always the case or if there are certain times and conditions associated with it. Maybe they say that if they're only going to be fifteen minutes or less late, it feels like you're keeping tabs on them too tightly.

Of course, you don't know how late "late" is going to be, so your anxiety kicks in immediately when they're not home at the usual time, and you have to *know* when they'll be home. But to your beloved, that feels like a noose around their neck.

So what can you do? You can get upset that your beloved is feeling confined and put upon. You can escalate your emotions, but if you do that, you've got a fight on your hands. Or you can get curious and see if there is a way to solve the problem that will be okay for both of you.

Can you compromise in this situation? What would be a good compromise, and how would you state it? Again, ask for what you want: "Thank you for explaining that. Okay. Then I would like you to call or text me if you're going to be more than twenty minutes late." You've given an extra five minutes, and if your beloved is going to be later than that, you want them to call or text you.

Be willing to let it go. Let's say that in this case, your beloved says, "Yes, I can certainly do that."

You've just had a positive discussion. No one got upset or ran out of the room, and you both feel good. Life goes on.

But it's always possible you're not going to get what you want. There are lots of reasons for that, again having nothing to do with you. People react from their learning, training, and childhood. It's not your job to change anyone. It's your job to be okay within yourself to let the object of your affection be who they are.

By using this technique, you can have a decent discussion without it getting out of hand. In a good marriage or partnership, a compromise or change can usually be brought about. It takes some work and effort, but that's why you're here. You're committed to this process.

And commitment is about the long haul.

THE LONG HAUL

One of the hardest things about changing your life is that it takes so darn long. Or at least it appears to. But let's take a look at this.

Let's say you're thirty-five or forty. That means you've been cultivating your current habits for thirty-five or forty years. You probably didn't start out at the level of anxiety you're at now. It builds up over time—sometimes quickly and sometimes more slowly. So let's say it's taken you thirty to thirty-five years to get where you are right now. Older folks (like me) have got even more accumulated habits to transmute

But don't despair. You're not going to change that in two days or two weeks. In two years, you might be making some inroads. You're developing new habits, and the trick is keeping the habit going. Somewhere along the line, you're going to say, "I've been meditating, being mindful, and taking care of myself for some time now, and I don't see anything happening. I'm still having problems. Why should I continue? Life was easier before I started this."

Was it? It was certainly more familiar. But was it easier? Or was it full of anxious moments, doubt, fear, a feeling of being totally out of control and unable to think straight, and wondering if you were losing your mind? Be honest with yourself.

Like anything, change takes time, and it sometimes happens so slowly you can't see it. We sit in our skin and don't notice the changes. If you're still wondering what I mean, consider something I've seen with pets. Let's say you have a dog. If you're fortunate, your beloved dog grows up and goes through all of the usual life changes. Because you see your dog every day, you don't notice the little things. But a friend who hasn't seen your dog in several years comes by, looks at your dog, and remarks about the gray on his face and how his whole bearing seems different. He walks a little more slowly. His fur is a little rougher. He looks long in the tooth. You haven't really seen it at all, but the changes are there.

Five years from now, if you sit quietly and contemplate where you are versus where you were, I can guarantee you're going to see and feel a difference if you think back to when you started your journey to letting go of anxious attachment. How often did you feel anxiety when your beloved didn't text you right away? How many times did you pick up the phone and call or have a crying jag because you felt worthless or abandoned? How many times did your heart pound in your chest with fear? Five years from now, compare that with now. Even a tiny change is a change for the new. A change to a more secure you. You're in it for the long haul.

I'm not big on exercise, but I know that to maintain a good quality of life, I need to move my body. My idea of a good time is lounging on the couch with my feet up with a cat on my lap, reading a good book. This is not going to keep me physically fit (although it's great for my mind and the cat really enjoys it).

When I discovered *Yoga with Adriene* on YouTube, I found her personable and fun to watch. And she made yoga doable, so I began the habit of practicing with her. Every January, she does a thirty-day challenge. It's thirty days of yoga, and every day there's a new practice. She mixes easier stuff with some really challenging (and long) practices, and I'm here to tell you I wouldn't call it fun. It's definitely not in the same league as lounging on the couch with the cat and a book. *That* is fun. Add a bowl of potato chips and we're talking a serious couch party.

But doing yoga is satisfying. For at least four years, I tried and failed to do all thirty days of the thirty-day challenge. Every year, I fell flat on my face. There were days when my excuse for not exercising was as lame as the fact that it happened to be snowing. What? How does that have anything to do with skipping yoga? In my mind, it did. At the end of the thirty days, I felt like a failure. My commitment to the process was really lacking.

Then one year I grabbed commitment by the teeth and decided that no matter what, I was going to complete the thirty-day challenge, and I was going to do it in real time: January 1 all the way through January 30. I don't know what changed. Maybe I was tired of beating myself up because I didn't complete the challenge. But here's the thing: I did it.

Was it easy? No. My husband and I like to do yoga together, and there were some days when he was just too beat from his day job to look at Adriene and her downward facing dog. In the past, I would have used his weariness as an excuse to skip it myself. But this time, no. I wanted this *for me*. Out came the mat, and Adriene and I (and sometimes my cat) went through the challenge for that day.

During that particular period of thirty days, we took a trip to Arizona for some training for our coaching business. We drove. We brought our mats. I exercised with Adriene in a campground. At the end of a busy day of training, out came the mat, and I did the day's challenge. It was not fun.

But it was satisfying. I was a woman with a mission. I had promised myself that this time, I was going to do it, and nothing was going to get in the way of that purpose.

You can't believe the twists and turns my brain took as it tried to get me to quit. I decided that feeling good about myself was more important than anything else. And nothing was going to make me feel good about this except doing the challenge every day.

I completed the last day of the challenge and pinned my score sheet (a handout with each day's challenge you could check off as you completed it) on the wall in my office. I was so proud of having done *every* day. It changed my life. I knew I could finish something I started. Up until that point, I was terrible at completions. I was great at starting things. Completing? Not so much. But this time, I both started and completed something.

Once the challenge was done, I did take a breather from yoga. Then I'd fire up Adriene's show a couple times a week. Recently, I've gotten back into a steadier routine. It's gotten to the point where if I don't do yoga, even a quick ten minutes, at least five times a week, I physically don't feel well. I like how I feel when I make the commitment to myself and pull out my mat.

My upper body strength has improved. Something that has been a bit of a challenge has become effortless. It's kind of like when you're a kid learning to ride a bicycle. One day you need training wheels. Then maybe you need your dad to hold onto the seat to keep you steady without the training wheels as you ride. Then one day you're on your own. No training wheels. No dad keeping you steady. What had been a challenge is now effortless freedom.

As a kid, your commitment was learning to ride a bike. As adults, we continue to make commitments to growing, changing, and learning.

MAKING COMMITMENT WORK FOR YOU

You have a vision of what you want your life to look like. Great! Just know that it's not going to happen overnight, and the journey, if you allow it, will be just as exciting as the end result. When you're being mindful and being in the moment, every little thing becomes a big thing because that's all there is. You're not worried about the future and you're not dwelling on the past. You're just doing your thing.

I've given you stories about my journey, but your journey will be different because it's your journey. But if you will commit to yourself, even if you fall down and have to get up three hundred times, in the long run, it will be worth it. I've done it. So can you. My fall down and get up count is somewhere around twenty thousand, so hang in there.

So start by taking small actions with changes you know you can make. What would be a good action to start with? Make it tiny. Maybe it's taking a couple of deep breaths before you dive in to your workday. Just come up with something and write it down. Then do it. Every day. You could even make yourself a score sheet like my yoga thirty-day challenge score sheet and cross off the date every time you complete your task. You will be amazed how one small change can make a world of difference in how you feel about yourself.

Once you're comfortable with that first small change, add another one. Then another. Be easy on yourself, and give yourself the time needed for the changes to become second nature and something you do with ease and joy. If you try to go too fast, you could sabotage yourself. Here's an example.

Let's say you love to write, but you're very inconsistent in your writing. It gives you pleasure, though, and you have a lot to say. You're just terrible at finding the time to put pen to paper (or fingers to keyboard). So you decide you're going to finally write that novel that's been rattling around in your head for the last thirty years.

You decide to sit down for four hours every day and write the novel. Whoa! You're trying to go from zero (inconsistent) to sixty miles an hour (writing four hours a day) immediately. Instead, commit to something more attainable like thirty minutes or an hour one or two days a week. Make a score sheet for yourself and schedule the time to write on your calendar. Be sure to make that time you carve out for yourself a time that will enhance your chances of success. For instance, if you know that Wednesday evenings are usually free for you and evenings are a good writing time for you, schedule writing time for Wednesday evening.

Commit to doing it for as long as it takes to get a habit going. Maybe you sit down and begin journaling before you settle in and get to your novel. That's fine. Just make a date with yourself, sit down, and write. See how it feels. Do you look forward to your writing time or do you dread it? It may take a little talking to yourself the first few times to get into the groove.

It can be overwhelming to think about writing an entire novel, but when you take it one writing session at a time, the novel *can* get written. Truly, be easy on yourself. It's not easy to change a lifetime habit into something else. But if you take it in tiny steps, before long, you'll find yourself with a whole new habit because you decided to commit to yourself and to the process.

The biggest mistake people make when committing to something is trying to get to the end result too fast.

If you want to let go of anxious attachment, it's important to commit to the process. Improving your relationship with your beloved doesn't happen overnight, but with a long haul commitment, it will. The first step is to know who you are. The exercises and suggestions I've offered will help you with that. You may feel at first that you're unworthy and undeserving to be who you truly are. You *are* worthy and you *are* deserving. It's your birthright as a human being.

When I was bouncing from relationship to relationship, I was like a chameleon. I took an interest in whatever my beloved was interested in. I learned a lot about airplanes, classical music, car racing, and different religions. If it interested them, it interested me. I already liked some of those things, but they weren't as important to me as they were to my beloved. I had to learn what *I* liked. In any relationship, it seems to help to have some commonality. I'm not religious, but I am spiritual, and one of my many relationships was with a man who believed that when you died, that was it. No Higher Power, no moving to the next thing, no veil to cross. That was a pretty big gap, and it was an important one. Having some commonality with the big things in your life, whatever those are, is a good thing.

The next thing to learn is that while commonality is great, it's okay to have your own interests. That's part of being who you truly are. For me, it's horses, and for a long time, it was riding, taking lessons, and going to the occasional horse show. My beloved likes horses because they're beautiful animals, and they're instrumental as part of our coaching business, but he has no desire to ride. That we didn't share that particular passion had to be okay inside me. I went through a lot of hoops in my mind before it became okay. Using the techniques I've shared here helped a lot. I was able to let go of my anxiety about Glenn not wanting to go to the barn with me, and I was able to allow him to do his own thing, knowing that just because we were separated didn't mean our relationship was falling apart. It took a long time to learn how to let that separation anxiety go.

Being a chameleon only gets you so far. So does being a doormat by being agreeable at all costs in an effort to make sure the relationship is always smooth. It doesn't work that way. Over time, disappointment and resentment creeps in, and then the person with anxious attachment is even more anxious because that can be felt at every level. You have to draw a line in the sand (a thing someone with anxious attachment hates to do) and trust in yourself and what is good for you.

One of the things that really woke me up was my cat. I had a lovely cat who had been with me longer than any of my relationships. Her name was AC (for Additional Cat). Where I went, she went. I met and got involved with a man who, to put it nicely, put up with her. She always slept with me. She was my pal. She was my confidante. He never said he was jealous of her, but over time, I realized that was the case. When we bought a new house, he said he no longer wanted her in the bedroom with us because he didn't like fur on the pillows. He also seemed to resent every moment I spent with her, which wasn't that much in the grand scheme of things. He didn't like anything that took my focus off him.

Someone who was strong within themselves, who wasn't trying to keep the relationship "happy" at all costs, would have said, "I'm sad you don't want her in the bedroom because she's very important to me. What else is there about her being in the bedroom that bothers you?" A conversation would have ensued and a compromise found. Did I say that? No. I knuckled under and agreed that AC should stay out of the bedroom.

AC spent a lot of time at night outside our bedroom door crying. I hated myself, but I didn't have the strength to challenge his wishes. When my husband went out of town, AC and I spent all our time together, including in the bedroom at night. I would wash all the bedding before he returned. This is no way to be in a relationship. It's deceitful. It's disrespectful. It was not loving.

There were lots of other things about the relationship that were not good. He compared me to his ex-wife. He wished I was thinner. He didn't like how I talked with his daughter, although his daughter and I felt we got along fine. And remember, this was at the height of my anxious attachment, so every remark he made, however innocuous, went into the folder marked "My Faults." It was not a good situation for either of us. Eventually, I got strong enough to leave the relationship, and of course, AC came with me.

I learned a lot from that situation. I learned that it was okay to say no if I disagreed, and if I didn't, I was hurting myself and the beings I loved. I learned that it was okay to say what I wanted, even if it was difficult. It was my very first baby step to letting go of my anxious attachment.

So when I met the person who was to become my last (and best) husband, Glenn, I told him right up front, "I have a cat. She sleeps with me. If that's a problem, we're done right now." It was hard to say because I really liked this guy. But it became more important to me to say what I needed and wanted and to protect my furry friend than it was to be anxious about whether he would like me and my cat. It was early in our relationship, and for me, it was a turning point because I said what I needed.

I didn't say it elegantly and I didn't use the tools outlined in this book because at the time, I had no tools. I wouldn't approach Glenn or anyone else with this sort of ultimatum now. We learn; we grow. At the time, it became easier to deal with a potential problem right up front than to assume, hope, or make up stories (which is what our brains do to us).

Glenn, who had not had a lot of experience with cats, liked me enough and liked animals enough to say he was willing to go along with that. Score! I said what I needed to say, inelegantly, and survived. For me, it was a start down the road to wholeness and loving myself. We now have five cats, and when it's really cold, we joke about how we could use a couple more to keep us warm.

It really pays to say what you want and what makes you happy instead of being so anxious about being loved and cherished that you will do anything to make the situation "right" for the other person. That's what getting to know yourself and being calm and centered within yourself will do for you. And to do that, you need to commit to yourself. And that takes time. It is, indeed, a long haul.

That one situation with my darling AC started me on a path to wellness. I started to notice my patterns. Believe me, I didn't get rid of them in one fell swoop. I can't emphasize enough how long this can take. Three steps forward, two steps back, was a dance I did with myself for years. But each little commitment I made to myself helped me make a big commitment when it mattered the most—because I almost killed my marriage to my beloved, Glenn, by allowing all my patterns to resurrect themselves.

My biggest pattern was to walk away from difficulty in shame. I couldn't make it perfect, and the anxiety and asking for validation from the other by always being in touch and always trying to make myself into what the other person wanted wasn't working. So I would start to look around. That started happening about three years into our marriage.

Glenn and I separated for a while. He went to another state because we were thinking about moving there, and he went ahead to find a job and a place to live. That was the story we told ourselves, anyway: Everything was okay and this was the next best step. But basically, we were not in a good place. It could have ended in divorce.

But here's where a miracle happened. He decided to come back. He left Colorado and moved back to where we'd been living together. He actually gave me the validation I was looking for because his returning told me I was worth something to him. And I was far enough along in my own self-growth to recognize it. If I had been deep in anxious attachment, I would still have questioned everything, and I could have made it worse by being even more clingy and needful. But all the work I'd done on myself to look inside, keep myself calm, and understand that I was worthwhile and worthy was starting to do its job. And I began to believe.

The turning point came on a plane trip to New Orleans, where I was going to attend a technical conference with some colleagues, one of whom I had become involved with. On the plane, I realized I was at a crossroads. I could continue down the old, familiar path, or I could stop and realize what I had.

Why would I give up a guy who made me laugh, who loved my cats as much as I did, and who had enough interests similar to mine for a guy with a cute accent who wanted my cat to stay outdoors? (There it was again. I owe a great deal to that cat.) In the past, I would have assumed I knew best and would have continued down the path of least resistance—the shiny new relationship where the two of us were always in touch and always lovey-dovey, where

I was always feeding my anxiety with what I considered love and consideration.

That path did not produce a sustainable relationship. I didn't have to look at or love myself. I was getting all the good feels from outside myself and lots of confirmation that I was loved and lovable. I was unable to commit long-term to anything, including myself. I was unwilling to look at the bad with the good. It felt normal to be anxious and need to be connected to someone every second, and if I wasn't, then there was something wrong. But that whole scenario was unhealthy.

I realized I had never made a deep commitment to anyone or anything. I was always giving up who I was for someone else. I knew that it was risky, but I was worth a good, solid committed relationship.

It scared the crap out of me.

And I knew I wouldn't be able to look myself in the mirror if I didn't make a huge change. It would just be the same old thing, over and over again.

I chose me.

While I was on the plane, I wrote my husband a letter telling him of my commitment to our relationship. It was a very big commitment, and all the little commitments I had made to myself along the way helped me get to that point.

Even so, there have been sticking points along the way. I get triggered, I react, and then we talk about it. My husband has his own stuff, and he gets triggered too. But because we're committed to each other and to our relationship, we sort it out and continue on. And the next time the trigger happens, it's usually not so bad.

We have way more good days than bad, and we laugh a lot. We have learned to give each other room to grow and be who we are, and because we're committed to the relationship and to each other, we've been able to navigate our way through a lot.

We meditate. We take long walks in nature. We allow each other space to be quiet and go inside. We keep in touch, but in a good way rather than a scared way. We've been married for over thirty years, and we've just scratched the surface. We have *commitment*.

NOW WHAT?

The bottom line is this: Never give up. If letting go of anxious attachment is worth it to you so you can have a great relationship, commit to it and it will happen. It may not happen overnight, but it will happen. To have a great relationship with someone else, you need to have a great relationship with yourself. And that's the thing you want to never give up.

Listen to what your body is telling you, using the techniques you've learned here. You will never go wrong if you're honest with yourself and listen to what your body and heart are telling you.

If you've been working at letting go of anxious attachment, both on your own and through the seven hacks I've provided, you've already done a lot. And at the same time, it may be merely a start. It takes a lot to become the person you want to be: happy, fulfilled, calm, able to take things in stride, and happy within yourself. You may need additional help. I invite you to look for it and embrace it. Nothing is done in a vacuum. People need people.

Find someone who can help you. Consider joining a support group. Everyone is unique, so explore and find what works for you. That might be therapy, equine assisted coaching, a class in meditation, or some other form of healing work. If nature is important to you, spending time in nature can be a great adjunct to the process. If animals are important to you, spending time with your animal friends can also be a great help.

The most important thing is that this is for *you*. It's not for your beloved, your neighbor, or people you think you need to impress. It's for *you*.

You are incredible, and you have started on a path that will change your life.

Here's to *you*!

ACKNOWLEDGEMENTS

This book wouldn't sound this good without my editor, Melanie Mulhall of Dragonheart, who took out all the fluff and unhelpful meanderings and helped it be a professional work instead of a messy first effort. Veronica Yager then took the perfected manuscript and gave it beautiful life in layout and design, for which I am grateful. Melisa Pearce, the founder of Touched by a Horse, was instrumental in helping me find my true self, as was my coach, Peggy MacArthur, and all my fellow herdmates. And to my beloved Glenn Weissel, I hope our adventure never ends. Thank you for being there through the last thirty plus years of good, bad, and mediocre.

ABOUT THE AUTHOR

Ashara Morris spent the first forty years of her life confused about who she was and how she should act with other people. She had a great childhood, but somewhere along the line, her sense of self got completely lost. She knows what it's like to be anxiously attached.

After many years of self-loathing, she met her beloved, Glenn, and that's when the work really began. She knew if she didn't change, she'd lose the best relationship she ever had. Ashara has used all the tips and tricks in this book and found them useful in building esteem and allowing her to be loved for who she is, not who she thought she was supposed to be.

Ashara is a Certified Master Gestaltist and animal communicator. She and her husband, Glenn Weissel, are cofounders of Harmony's Heart LLC and The Enlightened Squirrel Healing Arts Center. The work never ends. It is now conducted within a great relationship on a farm with multiple cats, dogs, and horses where nature is close and loving herself is closer.

CONNECT WITH ASHARA

Ashara Morris is a Master Gestaltist, Certified Equine Gestalt Method Coach, animal communicator, and shaman with a variety of offerings for those who want more.

Individual and Group Coaching
Individual and group coaching is offered both with and without horses. If you want to work on your anxious attachment and other life challenges in a nurturing, supportive environment, this is for you. When the horses are involved, it takes on a whole new level of experience. You can find Ashara at www.HarmonysHeartCoaching.com and email her at Ashara@HarmonysHeartCoaching.com.

Shamanic Work
Shamanic journey work is a fabulous way to get to the basis of your anxious attachment (and other life issues) in a safe and loving environment. You are never alone when on a shamanic journey. Doors open, experiences are revealed, and with knowledge comes ease. Discover more at www.HarmonysHeartAnimals.com/Shaman.

Animal Communication

Our animal friends know us better than we can imagine, and they have interesting insights into our lives and their connection to us. This isn't about Fluffy's food. It's about how you and your animal companions are working together for a better life for each of you and for a better relationship between you. Ashara offers individual phone sessions, group Zoom gatherings, and classes, both in person and via Zoom, in how to talk with your animal. You can also discover your power animal! For more information, check out www.HarmonysHeartAnimals.com.

Keynote and Other Speaking Appearances

Ashara is available for keynotes, breakout sessions, personal appearances at expos, and other speaking engagements. Her talks are always inviting, fun, and educational, and they cover a variety of topics having to do with Gestalt, coaching, and animal communication. She is available for your gathering and loves doing podcasts. You can reach her through www.HarmonysHeartCoaching.com and email her at Ashara@HarmonysHeartCoaching.com.

www.ingramcontent.com/pod-product-compliance
Lightning Source LLC
Chambersburg PA
CBHW071715020426
42333CB00017B/2284